COMRADE KING

This memoir relies most heavily on Khulu's memories of what happened during the course of the events we have recounted in the book. We have worked to make sure the content is as accurate as possible by checking original sources, journals, books, articles and newspapers as well as by checking the facts from those people who were also there at the time.

First published by Jacana Media (Pty) Ltd in 2023

10 Orange Street
Sunnyside
Auckland Park 2092
South Africa
+2711 628 3200
www.jacana.co.za

© Khulu Radebe and Jeff Kelly Lowenstein, 2023

All rights reserved.

ISBN 978-1-4314-2998-1

Cover design by Hylton Warburton
Editing by Isabelle Delvare
Proofreading by Russell Martin
Indexing by Megan Mance
Set in Adobe Garamond Pro 11.5/15pt
Printed and bound by ABC Press
Job no. 004065

See a complete list of Jacana titles at www.jacana.co.za

COMRADE KING

Khulu Radebe
and
Jeff Kelly Lowenstein

PRAISE FOR COMRADE KING

Jeff has enabled Khulu Radebe to tell his story in his own voice. And what a story it is. We follow Khulu through the 1976 uprising, Robben Island, the ANC underground, exile, the battles of the 1990s and his coronation as King. It is a foot-soldier's view of an extraordinary journey, told with open-hearted candour. It is full of surprises and insights. Despite all the tough experiences he describes, Khulu is a man who gives one hope and faith in the triumph of humanism over a lifetime of obstacles.
– Anton Harber, director of the Henry Nxumalo Foundation and professor of journalism at the University of the Witwatersrand

The stark truth: a story by one who was not only in the trenches, but in battles in Angola, against the Apartheid's arm and its proxy Unita. Here a South African youth of then, from Alexandra together with other youth from South Africa confirms in no uncertain terms that South Africa's Freedom was not free … no one must ever forget that; even when South Africa is free, it is still … Aluta Continua!
– Mongane Wally Serote, professor and South African Poet Laureate

Be strong. Don't break.
Mariam Radebe

CONTENTS

Acknowledgements		ix
The prophecy		1
1	Family roots and childhood in Alex and Diepkloof	3
2	Joining the struggle	27
3	Robben Island	43
4	Returning to Alex	81
5	Angola	113
6	Amandla	149
7	Returning to South Africa	169
8	Becoming a king	187
Index		201

ACKNOWLEDGEMENTS

I want to thank my family and Prof Jeff's family for giving us the time to work on the book, which has come into being from the past seven years of conversation. I want to acknowledge the friendship that developed during the course of this work.

Khulu Radebe

My first thanks must go to Khulu Radebe. It's been close to eight years since we first met at his coronation in November 2015, and during this time we have spent hundreds of hours together, becoming collaborators and friends along the way of chronicling his remarkable life whose story fills these pages. I'm extraordinarily grateful to him for his patience, insight, generosity, care and humanity. It has been my honor to work with him on this project. His lovely wife Margaret Radebe could not have been more gracious or warm during the years in which I arrived and spent hour after hour with her husband.

At the same time, in a very real way, this book has been nearly 40 years in the making.

My passion for South Africa began in the mid-80s when I was an undergraduate student at Stanford University. My initial foray into activism did not lead to the university's divesting all of its holdings, but it did spark in me a dream that I might someday visit Alan Paton's Beloved Country.

That dream came true nearly a decade later, when I participated in the Fulbright Teacher Exchange Program as a teacher and soccer coach at the Uthongathi School, a beautiful campus nestled along leafy sugarcane plants and within walking distance of the Indian Ocean in Tongaat. I met Vukani Cele, my exchange partner, at the orientation in Washington DC in August 1995, beginning what has become a lifelong brotherhood. He gave clear instructions to his friends before he departed to America to take me in as a brother. They did just that during that year and have continued to do so in the nearly three decades since. In November 2015, Tsepo Mahlaba invited me to attend Khulu's coronation and took me the following winter to his home to hear the story of the trials he went through before becoming king.

Many people within the Wits Journalism Department have assisted throughout the project, as have the colleagues and administrators at Grand Valley State University since I arrived there in 2016. The university's Center for Scholarly and Creative Excellence, School of Communications, College of Liberal Arts and Sciences Dean's Office, Faculty Teaching and Learning Center, Office of Undergraduate Research and Scholarship and Padnos International Center have given travel, book subvention, student research and collegial support. Bridget Impey and the tremendous team at Jacana Media have done outstanding work at each step of the process. Special thanks to Isabelle Delvare for her extensive editorial input.

My friends and family, far too numerous to name, have given all kinds of help, too. You all know who you are and know how grateful I am to all of you for helping to make this happen. I'm excited to celebrate our joint accomplishment together.

Finally, Dunreith. In the quarter century we've been together, she has been my coach, confidante, booster, critic, ear and best friend. In addition to helping me become a better husband, father, writer, storyteller and man, she's also played an immeasurable role in bringing this project to fruition. All of my love and gratitude go to her.

Jeff Kelly Lowenstein

THE PROPHECY

Before I was born, before she was even pregnant, my mother was told by a prophet in the indigenous church she attended that she was going to conceive a baby boy.

But this boy was not her child alone.

This child belonged to a nation.

This boy was going to be arrested, she was told.

Don't take it to heart if he's arrested, she was warned.

This boy is going to live a terrible life. He's going to fight, he's going to suffer, he's going to go to prison.

He's going to go into exile, but when he comes back it will be to lead the people.

And all the things he will go through are to prepare him to know the difference between right and wrong when he is king.

That is what she was told, and this is the story of what happened.

1
FAMILY ROOTS AND CHILDHOOD IN ALEX AND DIEPKLOOF

My father was born in Natal. He was a tallish man who had two wives. My immediate siblings and I come from the first wife.

I'm told that my father was very quiet, someone who did not want any noise. He never liked the kind of people who enjoy arguing. 'This is the house of the ancestors,' he would remind you. 'If you make noise, you are chasing the ancestors away.'

Dignified, clean, always the best dresser. That's how he was.

If you fought with him, he would tell you without hesitation when he felt you were wrong. If you were right, he would also tell you on the spot.

He would carry four traditional sticks when he fought another man physically over something. Two for himself and two for his opponent. If you defeated him, he would invite you to share a cold beer. 'What has just happened is over,' he would say. 'You have won the war. I will not hold a grudge.' He never held on to resentment towards any person. That is what my elder sister Mabel told me.

He also had great charisma and eyes that would charm you. I'm told that he was exceptionally good at charming women. Women would fall for him as easy as that. There was this saying that whenever he was in Johannesburg, men who worked and lived there would ask my father to take their visiting wives home to Natal because he was so reliable as a driver. These men had come to Johannesburg to work, and their wives would visit them there once in a while. My father would drive the kombi that transported them back to Natal when it was time for them to go back there. Those women always praised him afterwards, commenting on how 'humble'[1] his behaviour was. A lot of men were intimidated by him.

'Please do not interfere with our wives,' they would plead with my father. 'We need them still.'

I'm told I have the same instincts as my father.

ACCORDING TO A KEY family story, the High Commissioner or Consular General was stationed in Maritzburg on the day my father was crowned King of the Hlubi people. He was the one who pronounced my father King on behalf of the British. That evening, however, an old man found my father and warned him: 'If you sleep here, you are not going to see the sun tomorrow. Someone is coming to kill you.'

The clan of Langalibalele wanted him dead. They believed that they were supposed to be in charge of kingship and submitted a claim. They came after my father even before he was king, saying: 'Somebody else is supposed to be king, not you.'

But Langalibalele was not the appropriate heir to the throne. A British historian wrote that their claim was not legitimate because our family comes from the Upper or the main House, not the Middle House or the Lower House. We come from the rightful house and they cannot contest our right to the throne. The High Commissioner knew about this, which was why he had come to crown my father.

'You are taking the kingship back to where it belongs,' one person said on the day of the coronation. He was backing my father and expressing the opinion of many of those present. I heard about this many years later, when I was seated with elderly people who were talking about past events.

---

1 In South African English, this means politely reserved and self-effacing. It is considered a praiseworthy trait.

On the day of his ascent to the throne, some elders gave my father a traditional medicine in a cup to drink – a medicine used in our tradition when a king is crowned and initiated into his role. 'The day you have a boy, you will take his blood and mix it with this medicine,' they told him. 'He will become king.'

He took the extra medicine with him in a special container and waited for years until I was born. 'Now I can die because I have a successor,' he said after taking my blood through cuts in my cheeks and mixing it with the sacred muti.

After this ritual, he left for Matatiele in the Eastern Cape. From there he moved to Bizana, the home of Oliver Tambo in the same province, and then to a men's hostel in Springs on the East Rand – the place called Kwa-Thema today. He was hiding and changing location to avoid the group of people who wanted to kill him.

While in Kwa-Thema he met my mother, Mariam, who was from Swaziland, which is now called eSwatini. My mother had married at a tender age and had given birth to a daughter. Following her husband's death, the family she had married into performed the necessary rituals so she could be released into a new life of her choice, including one with a new husband. My grandmother, my mother's mother, later took and raised her daughter in Swaziland.

My mother's uncle was living in Kwa-Thema at the time. His real name is Albert Linda Hlatshwayo, and we called him UmKhulu. I was named after him.

I don't know how my father and my mother met. I think it was the gods' doing. My father explained who he was, and my mother told him she was from the royal family of Swaziland.

After my mother and father met, they had their first child, a daughter.

Then it was me, the only boy in my family, followed by three sisters.

ALEXANDRA TOWNSHIP (ALEX), the place where I grew up, was founded in 1912. We who settled in the Transvaal (the part that is now Gauteng) like to say that Alex is the mother of many townships, in the sense that the other townships in the region were largely created as a result of the forced removal of people out of Alex. Soweto, which had a strong influence on the man Nelson Mandela became, was one of those.

Alex was a highly cosmopolitan area from the start, with a busy mix of people: Zulus, Xhosas, Vendas, so-called coloureds, Indians, Chinese, everything. Zulu, or rather a combination of traditional Zulu and township Zulu, was the dominant spoken language. Embracing Alex's diverse ethnicities and customs was the order of the day. The people from Venda, who were entrepreneurial and ran most of the shops in the township, were the only exception. Many of them came from deeply rural areas. Shy to speak their language – Shangaan – in those days, they often preferred not to stand out and thus were absorbed into the dominant order.

Besides being an area of great diversity, Alex was a place of huge contradictions that I was only partially aware of at the time.

There was a sense of unity when I was growing up in Alexandra. Everybody from 1st Avenue to 22nd Avenue knew everybody else. A child in Alex belonged to Alex rather than to a certain family. Every parent was a parent to every child there. No child could misbehave outside their own home without being beaten by another parent. You would get beaten again when they delivered you to your home. There were property owners and tenants. Despite these differences, everyone belonged to one united family.

Yet Alex also early on became one of Johannesburg's headquarters of gangsterism. The names the gangs went by came from movies that were playing at Kings Cinema at 2nd Avenue and Plaza Cinema between 8th and 9th avenues. Each gang had its own turf, its own territory. There were different types of gangs, and you had to be wary of them all. The gangs started to block you if you went beyond the area from 1st Avenue to 6th Avenue. The Ten Slaughters controlled the territory from 7th Avenue to 10th Avenue. The Ten Slaughters did not beat you up; they slaughtered you. They came from the area where my wife lived as a girl. The Dirty Heroes reigned from 11th Avenue to 13th Avenue. The Young Ones owned the streets after that.

Some of the gangs had been there many years. The Spoilers

and the Msomis dated back to the 1950s and the 1960s. The Dirty Heroes and the Ten Slaughters were from the 1970s. If you were not one of them you were regarded as a fool, an unprotected bari[2] who was liable to be harassed. At 4th Avenue a group from a rural area called the Panga Men had formed a gang because they were themselves regularly terrorised. They had created the gang as an act of self-protection.

Some gangsters operated on their own. There was one individual who would burn people's faces by pouring acid over them. In these ways, Alex was not a united family, but a place that was very much about the survival of the fittest.

I grew up around all these people. While we all lived in the same environment, no one paid attention to me because I was from a poor neighbourhood. Except for the pleasure of terrorising me, there wasn't much they could extract from me.

The peri-urban police were there, too. There were a lot of Alex residents you would never find on the streets during the day because they were worried about being picked up by the police for not being at work. The peri-urbans would look for them in houses and yards. During weekends it was loud in Alex and other townships, but during the week it was quiet because of the peri-urbans.

Our hippies were regarded as vagrants, too. One policeman by the name of Sibeko, who was knifed during the 1976 uprising, used to parade the hippies he arrested all over Alex.

Many of these hippies played in music bands such as the Flaming Souls, the Movers and the Anchors. My aunt's friend, Short Ry, was a member of the Anchors. My other aunt's husband John acted as manager for the Movers. Sam, the Movers' drummer, later inspired me to become a drummer.

Alex had many single mothers and no electricity. We only had paraffin lights, so it was a dark city. The sound systems we listened to all used batteries. In some cases the men had moved away because they had decided to desert their families.

My father worked in the butchery in Alex for a while, and he would buy cheese, peas and milk from the butchery to sell to his

---

2   Country bumpkin

private clients. He and my mother split up when I was very young. I was raised mostly by my mother.

She was short and soft-spoken, a quality my parents shared, and lived her life for other people. Possessing a sunny disposition, she was always smiling when I was young. She never drank any alcohol, was spiritual and prayed a lot, mixing traditional views of ancestors with Christianity. She was also a seer, someone who had spiritual visions.

After starting in a one-roomed house on 18th Avenue that we shared with chickens, we moved into a two-roomed brick house where my grandmother had lived at 130 4th Avenue. We went there after she moved from Alex to Diepkloof in Soweto. There was a bed in each room, which also housed a kitchen, a table and a chair in the corner. Although her new home was bigger than where we had lived, it was still very crowded. My mother, my four sisters and I stayed there. My mother's elder sister also lived there, with her four – then five – children, as did her younger sister and her two children. My mother's two younger brothers, who had four children between them, were there, too. Sometimes my uncle Albert from Kwa-Thema and my uncle Joseph Kiki from Rockville, Soweto, would bring their children to stay with us. Extended family would stay at my mother's place when they came to Joburg. You'd even have other visitors from Kwa-Thema. This made for even more mouths to feed.

Everybody would be in that house at night. We children would all sleep together on the floor. It was very cold in the winter, but you would never feel very upset about it because you were a child.

My mother dealt with her life with enormous self-reliance. Samuel Radebe, my maternal grandfather, could have helped, as he used to own property. But he didn't want anything to do with my mother. He had never wanted her to come to Johannesburg in the first place and had been furious when she'd brought all of her siblings from Swaziland to live in the city. When asked why she had done this, she explained that my grandmother's younger sister ill-treated them and that she needed to protect them from her.

Ironically, when my grandfather took ill many years later, my mother was the one who provided him with a place to stay and cared for him before he died. I used to take him to the outside toilet, start playing with my friends on the street, and forget that I'd left him there. After hearing him shout from inside the cubicle, I'd fetch him and walk him back to the house. He'd carry on at first as if nothing had happened before making me lean down as if to tell me a secret, grabbing my ear and saying, 'Don't leave me there again!'

From before I was born, my mother worked for Farm Fare – a company that packaged chicken. She would also buy boxes of frozen chicken from them and divide the carcasses into portions of five or ten pieces to sell at a small profit. In those times, a whole chicken cost between R1.50 and R2.00. As a young child I would go to every house in the area, knocking on doors and telling people that we were selling chicken. We worked from hand to mouth; and didn't have much of anything.

'I'm disappointed in your aunt,' my mother confided in me one day. My aunt had gone to the manager at Farm Fare, a white man, and told her that Mariam was stealing chickens and feeding a lot of children with them. Since my parents had split up at this point, my mother was the breadwinner at home. My mother had recommended my aunt for a job there, and she had betrayed my mother by trying to get her fired from work.

The manager asked my mother how many children she supported, and she told him. 'Are you sure that woman is your sister?' he asked her on hearing her reply. 'I'm going to give you two boxes for free, because you are doing a great job of feeding so many people.'

We had a happy home despite our circumstances. As younger children, we never took proper notice of having so little. Our limited clothing was certainly a clear sign that we were many in the house. My mother often wore her uniform from Farm Fare. I used to wear the same black jersey and black trousers day in and day out and was still wearing the same clothes in a larger size years later. Naturally, there was always someone at home to benefit from my hand-me-downs. When I was older, people used to say that I was in mourning for the kids who had been killed during the uprising of June 16 1976. I would go to school, come back and wash my jersey and trousers in the evening. I had one or two pairs of shoes but went barefoot at home, keeping my shoes for school or formal occasions. We all grew up not wearing shoes – whether inside or outside the house.

I had an Afro comb that I wore *in* my hair, but never combed my hair because I didn't feel like it. I was very much into cleanliness, though.

We had bread and tea as our staple food, because it was cheap. It's a staple for me still today. I like it because it's filling and inexpensive. I don't remember experiencing severe hunger. When my sisters ate from my portion of food, I would tell them to continue eating. I would stand up without fighting and just walk away.

We'd just have black tea; milk was a privilege for us. I'm told by my siblings that I used to like sugar as a child. That sugar would become glucose and give you energy. We had a lot of sugar in our tea, so we had something sweet even though our life was hard.

My mother would come back from work and say, 'Who finished the sugar?' It was obvious: we children had finished the sugar. She always asked anyway.

WE USED TO GET our water from a communal tap and used the bucket system to go to the toilet. We were like most other families in Alex in that way.

Some families around us were better off. The Moerane family, for example, was the only family in our area with a telephone. The Morgan family and the Makgale family both owned property, and the Ogen family lived in a 'Casino flat', so named after the owner. You could see that your life was lowly compared to theirs. You were nobody. You would not think of proposing to their daughter, you didn't belong in their league. They would never have accepted you. The Lifakane family on 2nd Avenue was one of those families.

The rest of us were just nobodies. I later rose up in Alex society because of my political involvement. People started to take serious note of me after I came back from Robben Island. But when I was organising following the June 16 uprising, people looked down on activists. I was regarded as someone who would not take a bath. They called me a *vuilpop* – an Afrikaans expression meaning a 'dirty person'. Certain people, like the property owners who belonged to the Alexandra Property Owners' Association, would act like I was a dirty bastard because I was helping to organise the community. 'Who is he to talk to you?' they would ask other people.

After I came back from Robben Island and the ANC was unbanned in 1990, people in the community started connecting me with my maternal grandfather, Gaur Radebe, who had been Nelson Mandela's mentor. To a large extent, they listened to me because of the respect Gaur commanded.

I was well aware of that, but at least it was an improvement on my days as a kid and a teenager in Alex, when I stammered consistently. I don't know for sure why I stammered. I think it was probably the result of an inferiority complex because our family, despite its fortitude, was always in danger of being despised for reasons beyond our control.

At school I would sit at the back of the class to avoid being made to engage, for fear I might stammer and expose my weakness. Kids would laugh at me when I spoke and make me feel bad about myself.

This reticence persisted as I grew older. Even though I had my own carefully conceived views, I would concede that people I was arguing with had a point even when their arguments were wrong. That fear may well be why, as I became increasingly active politically, I was more comfortable organising from behind: acting from the wings as the brains of the operation. I preferred to be on the UG, the underground level. The more comfortable thing for me, at the time, was simply to pass on the credit. In contrast, Obed Bapela – born in Alex in 1958 – was the kind of person who thrived at the front of the stage.

I realised in prison that I would have to learn to assert myself and articulate my beliefs. Being able to study through correspondence in jail helped me a lot. There was also Gumi (full name Ngomso), my personal tutor on Robben Island, who hailed from New Brighton, a township in the Eastern Cape. He made me feel I had value and trusted me to find the words I needed. He had been arrested for trying to undermine and overcome the South African government. A teacher by profession, he knew how to encourage a student.

As a child, I did not spend all my life in Alexandra. I spent a lot of it at my maternal grandmother's house in Diepkloof. Her maiden name was Sophie Hlatshwayo, and she had married into the Radebe family. She was a very kind person who took me in when I was about two months old. I called her Gogo and Mama because that's who she was to me. She was a giant of a woman: rather fat, very strong, dark-skinned and with reddish eyes.

Gogo was the best dresser around. She would dress neatly, the way the Queen of England dressed, and cover herself in a Scottish blanket of many colours.

Although Gogo was friendly, she would fight with me and give me work to do whenever she saw me idling. Once she told me to work in the garden and I started talking to a girl. 'You see this bastard,' she said. 'I'm giving him something to work on, but he's talking to this girl.'

Gogo liked her gin and would sing about her original home of Swaziland when she drank: 'SD Swaziland, that's where I come from.' She was happy then. She and her associates, who were large like her, used to drink gin together and cover themselves in blankets. Several bottles of gin were hidden underneath those blankets.

One day I went with her to buy some gin and she made me carry the bag with the bottle in it. I didn't know what was in the bag, and, not realising its fragility, broke the bottle by mistake. 'You will survive because I like you,' she said. 'If I did not like you, I would have slapped you with a heavy *klap*.'

There were many women I remember from those times in Diepkloof. Ma Tshabalala was my grandmother's best friend. Cousins from the Sibeko clan, they would often sit together. When Ma Tshabalala stayed over, the next morning they would prepare and start the coal stove together at 6:00 am. The stove would quickly get hot and warm the house.

Violet, my grandmother's younger sister, used to visit from Swaziland. She was well known there as a seller of good-quality marijuana and was referred to as 'the one who is sharper than most'. Born into the Hlatshwayos, she had married into the Mgwenya family. People respected her in the rural areas of Swaziland, largely owing to her being the accomplished Sophie's younger sister.

Sophie had gone to Joburg and was well known as a shebeen owner in both Alex and Soweto. The rural people were afraid of her because of these accomplishments.

Even though I continued to live and go to school in Alex, I would go to Zone 2 in Diepkloof to see Gogo every Friday.

My grandmother never harassed me. She liked me very much. She did not make a fuss even when she found out I avoided school. But sometimes she would send me into unfriendly terrain to buy samp or mealie rice in an area that was beyond the Zulu section of Zone 2.

'Don't buy it just anywhere. I want you to buy it *there*,' she would tell me. '*There*' was not to her cousin's supermarket, the largest one in the area. She sent me instead to a hostile stronghold in the Shangani section of Zone 2 that stood next to the Wesleyan church she attended.

Once I had done that, my job was to run with the samp from the store to Dr Mchazo's surgery, which represented the border between the Zulu section and the Shangani section of Zone Two. Those Shangani boys would chase you up to the border but no further, because they knew it was unfriendly terrain for them on the other side. Still, the border was several hundred metres away.

'Mama, I can't go there,' I would tell my grandmother. 'It's a no-go area. They will beat me. They will kill me.'

'I'm going to stand here outside,' she would reply. 'I am going to look at you. If you go to Zone 5 to buy the samp, I will send you to return it to the shop. If you go to Zone 2, I will accept it.'

She would look at me intently with her brown eyes and say, 'I'm going to follow you. Don't bullshit me. I'm going to be watching you.'

'THERE IS A ZULU BOY HERE,' the Shangani boys would say when I stayed in Diepkloof. They could tell I was Zulu based on the area where I stayed and appeared to register my presence there as soon as I arrived.

I couldn't come out of the supermarket right after buying the samp. While you – the outsider – were in the store, they would galvanise, forming a tight mob to hunt you down. I also knew from past experience that the size and power of this gang could be rapidly increased by calling on siblings and other kids hanging out in the area.

Inside the store, I would analyse how I was going to manoeuvre out of the situation by considering how many of them were waiting outside. At moments like these, you are tense, scared and trying to find a way through. You are strategising to give yourself a chance to get through the gauntlet – and away.

When I came out, they would throw sticks and rocks at me – whatever weapons they could find. I would endure this and push one or two of them away before I took off – concentrating on the ones who were closest and carrying belts and sharp wire. After that, I had no choice except to run like mad, zigzag between them and outrun them. I always ran barefoot because that was easier and more efficient for me.

You are sprinting like hell because you know that you are finished if they catch you. One day, as I was sprinting with an ally, a guy chased us with his Valiant. He nearly hit us, this guy. 'Catch those boys!' he shouted as if we were thieves as he chased us with the car.

LUCKILY FOR ME I was a soccer player and fit, and I could run fast. Sometimes you would get a hot *klap* – they would manage to hit you as you flew past them. But they never caught me, and I never fell.

My teammates nicknamed me 'Goldface', after the main character in a '60s superhero film. Even today, when some of them see me, they say, 'Goldface, how are you?' I grew up with that name, and I used that speed to survive. My other nickname was 'Magwegwe', because I was strong and bow-legged.

Of course, I was finished when I got back to the house, gave my grandmother the samp and her change, and fell into the grass. The other boys would ask me what happened and I would tell them after I'd caught my breath.

I had to go to that store many times. I don't know why my grandmother wanted me to do that. Maybe it was her way of saying, 'Go and fight so that you can become stronger.' Perhaps she was instilling in me the discipline of fighting for myself, of not giving in to anything or anyone. I guess she was making me strong.

Somehow, the fact that she sent me to an established danger zone on all those occasions never made me *not* want to go to Diepkloof to spend time with her. Maybe I would have decided to stop going there if I'd been a different child. I didn't respond that way.

I ENGAGED IN OTHER, less frightening activities that built our characters as we were growing up. Most of the kids in Alex were trained by the Shukokai Karate Club, which met at the Alexandra Community Health Clinic. Maybe this was a result of the influence of the martial arts movies in vogue at the time. I remember that there was a black guy who had trained in Japan and had a black belt. He was a 'Sensei from Soweto'.

There was a truck driver named Simon who was a blue belt and used to deliver sorghum beer in Alex. He became our instructor. Kids trained with him every afternoon. Simon and Vusi Ndlovu, who was a brown belt, were the instructors for the youth. Both of them liked me. Adults came to the club during the evening, when Simon would join the sensei as a student.

I was just a small boy when I started. (I remember I was still at the Jewish lower primary school called MC Weiler.) We used to do exercises first: mawashi geri, side kicks and kata.

I broke away from karate because I preferred the consistency of kung fu, as portrayed in the movies. (Many of the movies we watched were more Chinese than Japanese.) I was aware that a room at the Roman Catholic church was used as a training place for kung fu. A coloured chap was the instructor.

We never used the Japanese gear. Instead, we trained in red tracksuits like the ones Bruce Lee wore. You could also get a black suit with white socks, a Chinese t-shirt and black shoes. My mother paid for the tracksuit on installment as a special gift. I would go and pay the deposit for the clothing at a shop in Bree Street in central Johannesburg, which used to sell all that stuff.

Kids would dress up like Chinese fighters and behave like those characters in the movies after they laid their hands on the gear. I became one of the people in Alex who did that. Bruce Lee was the most 'in' thing in the townships, and people showed you respect when you wore that red tracksuit.

You would dress like the characters when you went to the Kings Cinema theatre for Bruce Lee movies. Everybody respected me because they didn't know where I got my clothes and would surround me during the interval.

In 1976, before I migrated from the Japanese school, the police chased a group of guys and me out of the clinic. We were doing shukokai, a specific style of karate. They did not want to see many people gathering together for any purpose. We moved from the Roman Catholic church to an area of open ground at the back of the Madala Hostel, before Nobuhle Hostel was built. We used to converge on the green grass in the evening, and old and young did karate together.

We later used the kung fu venue at the Roman Catholic church. After that, we moved on to Ntokozweni, where Vusi Ndlovu was the key person. We started having tournaments there, which included guys from the East Rand and Soweto. We would put up a stage for the tournament and battle it out for the trophy. We always won.

The majority of this group were young guys who went into exile and have remained bonded from that time up to the present. Even the instructor, Vusi, went and joined the Pan Africanist Congress (the PAC). He and I met for the first time after many years when I was in Bulawayo with the band Amandla. He was working for the Zimbabwean Broadcasting Corporation at that point and died of illness in Bulawayo some time later.

KUNG FU TAUGHT ME a way of conducting myself that has been of value to me all my life. I believe I need to continue to adhere to it on a daily basis.

We would start our exercises with a routine that was more of a prayer than anything else. We'd ask for faith and confidence, self-respect, sincerity, patience and understanding.

We would close with that same prayer. After that, we used to jump and perform a punch. Then we were done.

When I was doing kung fu I met Elce, a Chinese guy who was a shop owner on 1st Avenue, where the Indian shops are located now. He was one of a group of men who had come to South Africa from China because they wanted greener pastures. Elce sold hardware for home repairs, including a useful variety of screws.

I approached him at his store and asked him if he could assist me with kung fu. He didn't answer my first three requests. He behaved as if he were picking something up from the floor before going straight into an attack.

I blocked him.

'You're not bad,' he said. 'You've got a platform.'

Elce taught me for a couple of months, and I improved under his tutelage. I was then adopted by his son Norman, who suddenly jumped over the shop counter to challenge me one day. We started fighting hard at the entrance to the shop, beating each other up and doing much damage to each other and the stuff in the shop in the process. Even though Norman was pretty good, he had a tough time with me. He liked me from that day onwards. 'You and me are brothers,' he told me.

Watching the Chinese movies of the 1970s enhanced our kung fu foundation and skills. The discipline taught us to be focused and to organise ourselves. Following it enhanced all of our performances, and I moved from beginner to advanced status.

One day Elce called and said he wanted to talk to me. 'I want to introduce you to someone,' he said. He left Norman at the store and took me to an older Chinese man on 1st Avenue who was experienced at kung fu. Rather than going in through the front of the house, which had a shop, we walked to a room at the back of the building. Magazines and kung fu charts were everywhere.

Elce was much better at English than the old man, who started talking to me in broken English. He showed me some Chinese characters and some Chinese art, and told me that both were sacred to the Chinese.

I had to demonstrate that I understood the importance of what he was showing me. Some of the letters we looked at said 'punch and block', and the technique came from the characters.

'If you find a letter written like this, don't worry about what it says,' he said. 'Worry about what the technique says. The kung fu technique follows the letter.'

I used these techniques a lot because Alexandra Township was always there to test you. I found myself fighting one day on behalf of a fellow student called David Masondo. David came from Thembisa, and was quiet, down-to-earth and polite. Boys used to beat him every day when he came out of school. I asked them not to do that to him. One guy – a real bully – started to focus on both of us as a result.

'I'm going to beat you up after school,' he told David during the day. A lot of kids converged to watch what was about to happen. Adults on the street intervened, so the youths went into the yard of the Roman Catholic church to fight near the church building so no one could see them from the street.

I stepped in as children were waiting for David to be beaten. No one in that group knew that I did kung fu or that I was at an advanced level. The bully started to punch me in the face and said that he would fuck me up. I told him I didn't want to fight. 'You are the boss. I'm afraid of you,' I said.

He kicked my buttocks from behind as I was walking away with David. 'Who the hell do you think you are, pulling David away from me?' he asked.

I handed my books to Muzi Kubheka, my good school friend, and to someone I knew called Papa. All I said was: 'I can't hold on to this rubbish.'

I got close to the guy and started hitting him. He wasn't big, but I was angry because he was a bully. I made as if I was kicking him, when in reality I was just punching his nose. He started bleeding. After a while I left him to his own devices, and David and I walked away. The bully and his cronies never bothered David again after that.

People in the township started befriending me because they wanted protection in order to survive. Sometimes you had to kick a few people to be a respected protector. I used a lot of nunchaku (fight sticks) and kicks to instil respect.

I also used to fight battles on behalf of my sisters. There were guys who bullied my sisters, wanting to force them into relationships. Sometimes they would take my sisters by force, with the intention of raping them. I would kick their door open and beat them up. Till today, those guys respect my sisters.

MUSIC, WHICH CAME IN numerous guises, also shaped us during my childhood. As rough as things were in Alex, we were always surrounded by it.

I loved music from the first day I heard bands in the neighbourhood. I used to go and watch all those bands like the Flaming Souls, the Anchors and the Movers.

I would go and watch the bands where they practised, not where they performed. They played guitar, bass guitar, and some even played the organ. They would be focused on their music while having fun and telling jokes. Moreover, they used to wear bell bottoms and play soul music that was like a James Brown sound. It goes without saying that these bands and their musicians were incredibly powerful role models for us.

The Movers used to practise right across from a funeral parlour. That's where I met the singer Blondie Makhene, young as he was.

I would go with my friends and we would sit and watch them for ages. I would study all of the techniques the drummers used. Sam Thabo, the drummer for the Movers, really inspired me. He sported an Afro like American hippies had and played a red drum kit. I fell in love with drumming from watching those drums and the way he played them. I truly appreciated and admired what he used to do.

Even though a different person eventually taught me drums, Sam was an inspiration. We ended up being lifelong friends, even if at the time I was just a little boy to the band. I'm told he's somewhere in North West now.

I got to love the drums to the point where I decided: 'I want to be like Sam.' I would observe the band, go home and practise. I used to find great happiness in that.

When I was visiting the Movers with my uncle one day, I saw that Sam had a young boy with him who was playing drums and spinning the drumsticks. His name was Gerald Khoza, and he became the drummer for the Flaming Souls, the youngest drummer in Alex and South Africa.

My aunt Ntombi Radebe – that same aunt who had tried to get my mother fired from her job at the chicken factory – helped connect me to Dorkay House. That's where music was taught to children who didn't come from privileged homes. It was the only place you could study music as a black person. You would be thrilled if someone said you were going to Dorkay. It was a big thing you could brag about to your friends.

'No, don't worry: I'll pay for you to go to Dorkay House,' my aunt often said. 'I see that you like music. You'll go to America one day. I'm going to send you to school. You'll go to America when you finish your school. You'll play with the Jackson Five.'

I did make it to America eventually, but not through her. My aunt never paid for me, but in some ways she gave me a much bigger gift. Although I don't think she ever had the money, she did see the passion I had for becoming a musician. She believed in me and helped me become immersed in the environment that energised me.

Aunt Ntombi introduced me to the maestros of that time. She was close to all these guys. They would walk up to her and greet her. So they knew me, too. And because they knew me, I could go anywhere they went.

Over time, Sam became my best friend. Collins Mashego was a friend, too. The two of them were among the top drummers in South Africa. The newspapers rated them as the best at their craft at one stage. The two of them and others could frequently be found at my grandmother's house. My aunt is my grandmother's last-born, and the musicians used to come and hang around with her. That was another way in which they inspired me.

For all their friendliness, Sam and Collins didn't teach me to play. *That* was a guy from another band, who was working to uplift youngsters in the area around 4th Avenue in Alex. I was hanging out one day at the place on 4th Avenue where my friends used to sit and discuss politics after school. I was on the edge of the group as usual, not saying anything because of my stammer.

I saw one of the regular people on the street at that time of day approaching. I didn't know Fana Selepe, but I had noticed that he seemed to be aware that I was sitting on the outskirts of our small gathering. I had no idea who he was, or that he had a band, and had assumed that he was returning from a regular job.

As he arrived that day, he stopped and asked me, 'How are you? Why are you seated alone? Do you want to play music?'

'I'd love to play music,' I replied.

'Which instruments do you like? Do you want to play guitar, bass or what?'

'Drums.'

'We can go now and you can start learning properly from today.'

I was amazed, but said, 'Wait. I must ask my mom first.'

'What time does your mom come home?' he replied. 'I'll come back then.'

'At about six she'll be here.'

HE WAS BACK PRECISELY at six, and politely asked my mother whether he could take me to go and learn drums using real drums, not tin drums. I used to practise in those days with drums made of tins and tyre tubes. I would use two tins or three. I added steel cauldron caps to create the high hat. I put the environment together myself because I didn't have any money.

'That's what he likes,' my mother responded. She was always supportive of my wish to play music, but used to warn me: 'You know musicians. They end up being hopeless. They are womanisers. Don't make it your profession, make it your hobby.'

I went with Fana.

He opened the rehearsal room when we arrived at the venue, which was a corrugated shack typical of the times. That's where the band practised. At once I noted the red drum kit to the right of the space and went to sit there: 'Woo hoo!'

Fana started by showing me the disco beat: 'You play this beat. If you get that right, I'm going to teach you the second lesson.'

The opportunity to sit on a drum kit for the first time in my life was a dream come true. Despite my excitement, I struggled at first.

I could not play the beat even though it was simple enough. I tried again. It still didn't go well.

I'm left-handed and didn't understand that the components were on the wrong side for me. Neither did Fana.

'I'm going to lock the door,' Fana said. 'I'll open it when you're able to play what I told you to play. If you don't play it, I'm not going to open this door.'

He was not friendly. He locked the door and I was alone. I *was* playing, but I could not master the beat. Then a voice inside me said, 'Take the side drum and change these things around.' Deciding to trust my intuition, I took the floor tom to the other side; and the high-hat snare drum to the left. I started on the disco beat again, and it was as if I had been playing drums for years. All of a sudden, it was easy.

Fana heard the difference and opened the door. 'What is happening here?' he asked. He immediately understood what I had done. 'Never change the drums again in your life,' he declared. 'This is you now. Never change them back to the right. You're a drummer. We can celebrate.'

I've been playing left ever since.

I LOVED THE DRUMMING, but I still found keeping time difficult as I got used to sitting on a drum kit. Despite this, I progressed and spent some time watching the band practise.

I did not initially realise that Fana had a problem with his drummer, his younger brother, Dumi Selepe. The band started to practise at five. Dumi would arrive at seven. He would do this every day, and would even make the band wait until he finished slowly smoking a cigarette. Two and a half hours in total. Every single time.

Dumi acted in this arrogant manner because he had no competitor. One evening when I was there, Fana told the band, 'I have somebody who is going to play for us while Dumi is on his way.' That was me, a young boy whose legs could not reach the foot pedal. They had to find a smaller chair and to adjust it for me. They brought it down, then said, 'Sit down. Disco beat.'

That was the basis for all of the songs. If you could do it, you could do 10 songs, or even 15 songs … Disco was big in the 1970s.

That's all they wanted from me and that's what I played. I was still struggling to keep time.

Fana taught me, however.

His method consisted of using old broken sticks. If he threw one of his sticks at me, I knew that my timing was not correct and that my speed was dragging. He'd be playing keyboard and manage to throw a stick at me at the same time. He would not throw it in the general direction of the drums; he would throw it accurately at me. The minute I slowed down the beat, he would also issue verbal warnings that the song was about to 'go down'.

Fana showed me the importance of keeping time. When I played for Amandla years later, I started using a metronome to practise. When Jonas Gwangwa saw me doing this, little did he know that it came from having sticks thrown at me at a young age.

When Dumi finally arrived that night, he walked in and started trying to remove me from the drums. 'Move this young boy,' he ordered imperiously in Zulu, snapping his fingers.

'No, you are not going anywhere,' the other band members told me. 'Sit.' Then they told him, clearly: 'Whoa, Dumi. *He's* going to play the drums. Not you. Out.'

Dumi hated me after that. Even though he had been letting the other members down repeatedly by showing up so late, he blamed *me*.

THAT IS HOW I started playing in a band. Every day when I came home from school I would clean the house, finish my homework, fetch my sister's children from their kindergarten, and rush to play drums with the band on 4th Avenue. Band practice would start at five. I'd be there at four.

BOB MARLEY WAS BIG. Peter Tosh also. So was Jimmy Cliff, who came to South Africa. Everybody loved his song 'Many Rivers to Cross', which was the most famous song in Alexandra and Soweto for a long time. *The Harder They Come* was a famous album of his. I liked another, older one called *Remake the World* even more. It was from the mid-1970s and in it he sang about how too many good people were suffering due to the actions of a greedy few. In some ways, Jimmy Cliff was a little more political than Bob Marley. Bob *was* political, but Jimmy Cliff was more confrontational.

Motown was big here too. We played songs by all the American artists, like 'Paradise' by the O'Jays, 'Victim' by Candi Staton and 'The Sound of Philadelphia' by MFSB. We used to imitate those artists and play their songs. All of them.

Because we played music all around Alex, I ended up hanging out with the giants of South African music. Fana made the connections for me. They never gave me the opportunity to play the drums for them as a young boy, but I would be around them and even accompany them as they drove around in their cars. Collins Mashego was famous and beautiful. He and Sam would engage in a Battle of the Bands between the Anchors and the Movers. When they didn't have shows, you would find both of them at the homes of various members of our family, including my aunt and my grandmother, drinking tea, laughing and joking around. They needed to be seen as competitors by the public, yet outside the limelight they would throw well-intentioned jokes in each other's direction.

Over time I ended up playing with the same bands they played with, featuring as their substitute drummer. People started referring to me as 'that fresh young boy who plays beautiful drums'. Even though I was still maybe just 10 or 11 years old, many musicians came to watch me, and to assess for themselves this young person who was already playing drum solos.

I also played with greats like Kippie Moeketsi and Allen Kwela, who at the time were performing with Levi Phahle, the son of our school's principal. He used to play the piano and his performance was a combination of Spyro Gyra and township jazz.

Sam was a soul drummer, and as I played soul I grew into marabi. I was influenced by Banza Kgasoane and George Lewis and members of what was to become Mango Groove. Marabi was a particularly vibrant form of township music that forced you to move. It reminded me of a dog I'd seen with a shaking sickness. Marabi even developed a style of dance, and you simply had to play it to claim your place in township culture.

In other genres, Big Hennie's Band played our kind of much-loved African jazz that was influenced by marabi. Oom Hennie was the guy leading it. There was penny whistle music, too. If you didn't play that, you were nobody.

You also had to play Zakes Nkosi's music well because that was your ticket to acceptance. You had to think hard before featuring other, lesser-known artists you found exciting.

Our band used to play most of this music at weddings. I would play the snare drum and the kettle drum. Someone would hold the kit in place for me. We would accompany the bride and the groom as they walked and danced. Everyone loved it.

I figured out how to divide my time between these different types of music. I'd be called because a group that was imitating the Americans did not have a drummer. Some other guys would be saying they needed a concert to support a worthy cause. ('We must fight against colonialism.') Yet another guy would tell me, 'Hey, man. We've got a gig if you want to join us. We're playing marabi.'

I performed with every group that approached me. I played kwela music, marabi music, reggae music, African music and new wave music. I even played heavy metal.

You had to adapt and to act in a unique way around each group. You supported their style of music, and you behaved and performed as that style required you to. To be respected in those heady times, you had to be able to play in every genre around and perform all of the songs on the programme. There was no playing around.

That's what I did.

Of course, life in Alex was not only about music. We had to deal with raids and with violence from the peri-urban police that got us to start organising for what became the June 16 uprising.

2
JOINING THE STRUGGLE

During our childhood in Alexandra, our parents would be woken up by the peri-urban police between 3 am and 4 am every morning from Monday to Friday. 'Maak oop die fokken deur!' the young Afrikaner boys would yell while violently kicking open the house door and demanding to see passes and permits.

Our parents needed to have both a pass and a permit. The permit showed the police who was eligible to sleep in the house. The pass was a different type of permit for people working in town. It meant that they had the right to be in Johannesburg, at least while they continued to work.

A category 10A pass was for people who had been born in the area and had lived there ever since. A category 10B pass was less straightforward. With B, you had to ask the chief of the rural area you were born in to endorse you for work in the white areas. The category covered people who had been in the area for 10 years under one employer, or who had lived there for 15 years without breaking any law (including any pass law). A category C pass allowed you to be employed, but your employer had to provide regular proof that you were indeed working for them. A valid C pass held by a man also allowed his wife and children to live with him.

You would have to pay a fine of R90 if you were arrested. Those who didn't have the money would be sent to a farm to plant or dig up potatoes by hand for 90 days. People were given one rand per day for their labour on the farm, hence the 90 days.

A lot of parents would run away naked or skimpily clothed because their papers were not in order. They would flee to an area near Alex called Marlboro, which in those days we called Emjeri. It was an area that had been cultivated by a group of Portuguese farmers before being abandoned. One of the decaying houses had an underground prison with chains for slaves.

You would see a lot of parents coming back from hiding in Emjeri at around 6 am. Other parents would stay until 7 am at the latest, after which even those working close by had to move on if they didn't want to be late for work. Neighbours would lend them clothes to cover themselves and try to lessen their humiliation.

Coming across parents running naked in the streets as we were making our way to school or the local shops disturbed us. Their abuse violated the necessary sense of respect for adults that is fostered in children from all South African cultures, including, ironically, the Afrikaner one. Seeing your parent, or the parent of a next-door neighbour, naked on the street in fear of being arrested was simply not right. How do you relate to any parent you have seen naked?

The topic would come up every time we met at street corners. In 1974 and 1975 we took a decision within a growing sense of our power as young people: 'This is not right,' we said. 'If we don't fight against this thing, it will never stop.'

We started by organising ourselves in our own area. Another youth group from 18th or 19th Avenue did the same. That is how the core of our growing group started on its mission to oppose the apartheid state. When the uprising happened in 1976, we were already fully committed and ready. After 1976, we escalated our resistance.

I ATTENDED MC WEILER school from Sub A (now Grade R) onwards. After that I moved to the higher primary school called Pholosho Primary. Like my first school, it was connected to a Jewish school. They had the ANC colours in their uniform. Pholosho Primary's principal, whom we called 'Principal Phahle', was married to MC Weiler's principal. He was a very strict man who was always formally dressed and wanted us to speak proper English. We were scared of him and would hide if we saw him on the street.

Both of the Phahles' sons ended up going into exile. George Phahle, the older son, was killed during the Special Forces raid by the South African Defence Force on Gaborone in June 1985. George's wife, Lindi, was also killed in the raid. The Phahles' younger son, Levi, survived but was deeply affected.

A group of friends and I spent night after night at school. There was another group there who came from the other side of the township. During those years in the early and mid-1970s, we would stay up all night to catch up on our studies. We called it 'cross-nighting', and we had the principal's permission to do this. He knew that we wanted to study so as to be better prepared for life in the future. We all had different careers we wanted to pursue. I wanted to become a medical doctor at that point.

We would get to the school between 7 pm and 8 pm, and study by candlelight until about midnight. Then we would put the books aside and discuss how we could change the status quo in Alex and South Africa.

In the early morning we would rest for 10 to 15 minutes and hit the books again. Closer to the start of the school day, we would tidy up, wash and go to class.

In those days schooling in Alex ended in Form 3 (now Grade 10), and Forms 4 and 5 were in Soweto. The older members of our group would thus leave for Soweto early in the morning and only come back at night.

School was the only place in Alex where you could find some quiet. Our parents and others who knew what we were doing respected our wish to cross-night as young people who wanted to be someone in the future. Criminals never harassed us, and we never experienced any disturbance from within the community.

The only time I experienced a disruption was when I was arrested during Standard 5: an event that ended my official education.

WHEN OUR GROUP ENGAGED in political work, we would go to the people of Alex. This usually took place at the opposite end of Alex from where I was living. I grew up on 4th Avenue, and it was a long trip to 17th Avenue, where my friend Thami Sibisi used to stay. Crossing the many gang boundaries took a long time and involved taking many chances. It was a difficult journey, but I was able to accomplish it – and to walk back when we were done.

A vibrant young woman named Tso Tso who lived on the same site as Thami Sibisi was one of the revolutionaries who contributed to our group. Obed Bapela and Jingles Makgothi, who both stayed on 19th Avenue, were two others. We would get together there in 1976 and start engaging with other youth in the area. That's how we formed the June 16 Committee.

We also created the group called Khawuleza Cultural Ensemble (KCE). 'Khawuleza' means 'hurry up' in Zulu. Under the KCE platform, we started inviting poets and writers from different corners of South Africa like Prof. Es'kia Mphahlele. We started creating a space for resistance poetry and for cultural activists of various kinds who were opposed to apartheid and used culture to fight against it. Various art disciplines were represented in the Ensemble, including dance and music in the form of gumboot dancing and drumming.

Before long, we started organising students all over Alexandra. We also connected with students and cultural artists in Soweto, Natal and other areas of South Africa. Dikobe wa Mogale, now known as Dikobe Ben Martins, was our connecting point in Maritzburg. He later served eight years as a political prisoner on Robben Island and in Johannesburg Prison.

Many people from Soweto believe that the uprising arose purely in their area. That's not the case. Many of the students who played a key role in the uprising came from Alex and had to do their last two years of schooling in Soweto. Alex students were at the core of the June 16 uprising and, moreover, were a key reason why it started.

Another common opinion is that the June 16 uprising was about Afrikaans as the mandatory medium of instruction. It wasn't only about that by any means.

THERE WAS A LULL in activity during the 1960s, when the ANC and the PAC were banned after the Sharpeville Massacre. Things were quiet and the enemy was confident that it had crushed the resistance movement. Out of the lull, the students of the time turned to creating organisations.

The South African Students' Movement (SASM), an organisation of high-school students, was formed in 1968. SASM was central in organising school students and encouraging them to take action against the effects of apartheid. Many of its members were responsible for what can be called the June 16 movement of 1976.

At the tertiary level, students first tried to engage with the only two black affiliates of the mostly white National Union of South African Students (NUSAS) (the University of Fort Hare and the non-white section of Natal University College). When the interaction did not yield the desired results, the ANC veterans whom the students consulted and whose political education classes they attended, advised them to form their own union. The students came up with the concept, first, of a Christian student movement, then abandoned that to form the South African Students' Organisation (SASO).

Founded by Steve Biko in 1969, SASO was influenced by the philosophy of black consciousness and the Black Consciousness Movement (BCM), a grassroots anti-apartheid activist movement that emerged in South Africa in the mid-1960s. SASO was intent on helping students to acknowledge their intrinsic value and develop pride in being black. Efforts to assist with the welfare of black people and to build black-inclined programmes in townships also came out of the BCM. The Black People's Convention (BPC), which Biko helped found in 1972, had as its chief aim to foster black political unity and solidarity towards psychological and material liberation for black people in South Africa.

As an aside: when I was on Robben Island, there was a guy who did not understand the difference between a BP petrol station and the BPC; and who thought that the latter was fighting to organise BP stations!

Before long, many BPC-inspired students and student leaders had been expelled from their universities. As they started to become teachers in township schools, they began organising themselves and having conversations with their students. They conscientised the students and encouraged them to fight for students' representative councils (SRCs).

This was all before 1976. By then, SASM too was closely identified with the BCM. Tsietsi Mashinini, a charismatic SASM student leader, rose out of that energy. At the age of 17, he was able to bring conscientised students around to the concept of a Soweto SRC.

At the same time, apartheid was entrenching itself and the state was trying to enforce Afrikaans as the main medium of instruction in the country's schools. Students in what was already a strong youth movement started to resist that imposition. The older students were politicising the younger ones, encouraging them to fight for the right to an SRC and to find other possible ways of doing away with Afrikaans. The government refused to budge on the language issue.

The situation in schools had been building for years. 'We need to send a petition to tell the state that it cannot impose Afrikaans on us,' the student groups started saying. In 1976, Orlando High said, 'We're not going to accept this thing!' and its students started boycotting classes. There were students from Alexandra and Thembisa among them, and the Alex students were also part of the Soweto SRC.

A group of us created an Alex SRC. When we were cross-nighting, we would put away our books at some point and start discussing the problems with having the Afrikaans language as a medium of instruction. Emotions ran high. Inevitably, this discussion turned to the ongoing issue of our mothers running naked in the street.

Since we couldn't gather as a group because membership would have landed us in jail, we often met under the protective umbrella of the Khawuleza Cultural Ensemble (KCE). This was our necessary public face.

We saw ourselves as autonomous people who had brought back the protest momentum. But many in the community regarded us as dirty types who were opposing the status quo without good reason, or even as young people who were mentally unstable. 'Even the Mandelas could not fight the system, so who the hell do you think you are?' the adults who had given up on opposing the system would ask us.

Despite improved cooperation between groups – particularly

between secondary and tertiary students – we had never achieved a strong, unified student movement. The build-up to one came through the progressive student movement that led to the Congress of South African Students (COSAS) in 1979. The BC people who had organised from within SASO were in charge of this development.

As the middle of June came around in 1976, we said, 'Let's go and march and hand in a memorandum stating that we are not comfortable with writing mathematics in Afrikaans without being prepared for it.'

The purpose of our march, which was to begin in Orlando, Soweto, was to make a strong statement about our memorandum and petition. We planned to do this by gathering as many people as possible from the various schools in that area,

The peaceful march was supposed to end at Orlando Stadium. We were on our way there when we were suddenly given short notice to disperse, quickly followed by the hullabaloo of the effects first of teargas, then of live bullets. When we heard that students had been injured and killed, we responded by burning cars and township administration offices in Alexandra.

Hastings Ndlovu was the first student to be shot dead, before Hector Pieterson. But the main issue was not who was shot that day; it was that a student march had taken place to hand in a petition concerning student rights.

On 17 June, a select group met at the back of Alexandra Stadium at about 5 pm to organise the response we would make the following day. Students were dressed as if they were going to soccer practice. That was when people were given tasks and responsibilities: who was going to do what, who was going to give the speech.

'This is how it's going to be tomorrow,' we decided. 'Take all your books and pretend that you're going to school. We all go to school and we disrupt the classes. If we don't go to class, we won't have the same impact.'

The township was already organised and there was a great deal of tension around. Alex students doing their secondary schooling in Soweto, and students from the Shangani-language Bovet Higher Primary School that stood on the grounds of the Swiss Mission church, were involved. Groups from Pholosho Senior Primary, Gordon Higher Primary, Skeen Primary and the Lutheran School were present, too. The last group was from the coloured school at the corner of John Brand and 3rd Avenue. All those schools came together to present the memorandum that had not been handed over because the police had started shooting.

The morning of 18 June was very cold. We set off, with Toto Skhosana and Japie Vilankulu leading us. Japie started chanting: 'Are we afraid of them?', after which Toto yelled: 'Are we afraid?'

'No!' the marchers responded.

We chanted for a while longer before singing the sombre song 'Senzeni na?' ('What have we done?'). We did not care if we died.

As we continued to sing and march, we stopped at the Casino flat on 4th Avenue. Japie stood on the stoep, again asking: 'Are we afraid of them?'

'No, we are not afraid!' came our answer.

The whole march couldn't get to all those schools, so a predetermined group broke away at 6th Avenue to fetch the students from Gordon. Another breakaway group went to Skeen Higher Primary. The students at the coloured school who were supposed to join in the march remained stuck in the school because their headmaster refused to let them out.

We regrouped at the corner of 4th Avenue. There was no evidence of a police response. All was well. At that moment, though, a notorious black policeman named Sibeko who was known for harassing our parents drove through in a Datsun van painted in that greenish-brownish military colour. He was pulled out of the vehicle, kicked and stabbed. I don't know whether he was killed.

We turned right towards the Putco bus rank at 1st Avenue. Two white policemen were reporting for duty. When they saw the crowd of students, they drove on as if nothing was happening.

I caught sight of a police Valiant. Furious and wanting revenge for the events of June 16, I threw a stone that landed in the middle of the windscreen and broke it. The car sped away towards the police station. That was the first time a police car had been stoned, and the other students gained strength from that gesture. We marched down towards the coloured school because we needed those students to join the march.

The shooting began on 3rd Avenue. We dispersed and met at the Lutheran church at 7th Avenue that became the venue for Sub A and Sub B education. I remember that a student called Ntwaza lost the school bell for Alexandra Secondary when he threw it down in the chaos.

As we hid there, we started talking about a beer hall down the road. In those days, beer halls were symbols of oppression to many people, especially for those who were politically aware. 'Let's go and burn it,' we yelled. A lot of people went there, broke in and started looting. Some people reversed a bus into the venue, removed the safe and went after the beer in a big way. The march had turned from a student march into something else.

We next moved on to 12th Avenue, where some people broke into the welfare office next to the Jersey Joe Boxing Club and started giving out blankets. Some adults among the crowd covered themselves in the blankets and rolled on the ground as if they were kids playing. Meanwhile, from 12th to 8th avenues on Selborne Street there was suddenly a fierce battle with the police, who started to shoot without warning. I ran away as soon as this happened. 'I've played my role, let me go back home,' I told myself.

'THANK YOU, GOD,' my mother exclaimed when I got home at around 11.30 am. She had been looking everywhere for me because she thought I might have been one of the children who had been killed. She was angry with me, but I'd felt I needed to do my part. The following year we started holding commemorations for the events around June 16. They were most powerful in a Dutch Reformed church.

We continued organising the students after the uprising began. Knowing the streets of Alex so well because of our work as organisers was an advantage. Our role was to make sure that the struggle was alive and so we had to know almost everybody. We used to regularly remove the students from school, sometimes all the students and sometimes only the younger students. Principal Baloyi of Gordon Higher Primary agreed with our demands on some days and disagreed on others. We would fight him when he disagreed. Whenever he resisted, we would take out whatever we had in our hands and start poking him with it.

The government cracked down hard after June 16, but we kept protesting to continue the boycott. We had to let them know we were still fighting. In 1977, the army encircled the township during a raid. They cordoned off the whole area and no one was allowed to come out. The police arrested many people, including everyone who was found not to be working. They searched every home.

In spite of their efforts, they didn't manage to arrest people like me. The security police kept looking for us, so we hid anywhere we could. I had a dozen different hiding places.

They did find me the day we commemorated the anniversary of the June 16 uprising. The event was at the church between Selborne Street and 5th Avenue, what we now call Rev. Sam Buti Street. Rev. Buti opened his Dutch Reformed church to us and gave us a voice. We were dressed in black and wearing black turtlenecks to remember those children who had been killed.

It was a very peaceful gathering until the security police came into the church and disrupted the commemoration. There were a lot of them. I managed to reach the back of the church undetected and ran out through the door. I was nervous, but they didn't catch me because I was very quick and fit from playing soccer. It was extremely close. They might well have shot me if they'd had the chance.

They chased me close to the home of one of our unit members, where the lady of the house knew me. Because the police did not have my facial profile, they did not have the means to accurately identify me once I had split from the church.

I decided to hide inside the house.

In those days, our parents' homes all had the same layout and the same large coal stoves. I knew that, and I also knew where to find brushes and cleaning cloths. Taking off my turtleneck and chucking it into a bedroom, I grabbed what I was looking for and began to clean the house.

'Can I help you?' the woman asked the police calmly when they came to the door. They told her that they were looking for me, came into the house, located me and started pulling at me.

'No,' I said, trying to resist.

'Why are you pulling him?' she demanded to know. 'This is my son.' In those days adults had to carry passes, while youths did not.

They argued: 'No, we can see he's sweating. He was running.'

'No, he's sweating because he was cleaning,' she replied.

She stood by me and they left. That brave woman is still in the same house in Alexandra Township today. I saw her not long ago, when I attended a memorial service for one of the guys who was part of the Khawuleza ensemble. I hailed her after she walked into the service.

'Oh, mama,' I said.

'You're grown up now,' she answered.

'You still remember me?' I asked.

'How can I forget you when I stood for you?'

If I become rich, I must buy her a proper present.

WE GOT CHASED OTHER times too. On one occasion, three of us – Obed, Moss and I – were in the Methodist church in Alex. It was a Saturday afternoon and Bishop Tutu was addressing the crowd.

We were wearing kaftans and ANC badges with the wheel symbol of the Freedom Charter on them. We were the organisers of the event, which included an ANC flag rally. We had a large ANC flag with us.

The police came rushing into the church. We used the back door to get out as usual, then ran one behind the other up to Louis Botha Avenue. The police were chasing us hard. They were large guys with great energy, but they could not catch up with us because we were running for our lives. They wanted to arrest us *with* the flag because that would be evidence of opposing the government and furthering the aims of the ANC, an illegal organisation. We knew that capture could mean a ten-year sentence. For a while, we threw the flag between us through the air. Moss had the idea of throwing it on the ground to reduce the chance of our being caught holding it. Obed picked it up and we ran some more. He threw it to the ground and I took it.

The men were catching up to me. I knew I could not hold on to it any longer and threw it to the ground, realising that I might have to abandon it there.

The strange thing was that we were running in the wrong direction. We had not run into the crowded township where it was easier to lose oneself, as we would normally have done. I don't know what made us run towards the factories on the edge of Alex, which were enclosed by fences. This would allow the police to find and isolate us easily on a Saturday afternoon, when the gates were shut.

But somehow the police stopped pursuing us. I don't know what happened. Maybe it was the grace of God watching over us. But they just went away.

MANY PEOPLE IN THE FIRST level of leadership within our organisation were arrested, ending up imprisoned or leaving for exile. We who were the second layer of leadership had to take over. Unfortunately the state looked for us, too. We were all being targeted. Before long, some of the people in our level who managed to escape prison also left for exile.

The police were forever looking for us and arrested us all over the place. It happened to me at my mother's house. When she told me the police were in the area and that I should go to the basement to hide, I replied that I would be all right. They came soon afterwards. My mother had been right, but by then I was tired of running from the police inside my own community.

They placed those they arrested alone in a cell, without food or water. We didn't know what would happen to us. Some people were lucky to be arrested and charged during their raids. Others were detained and killed. But there was a woman who gave me courage. She sang freedom songs about Mandela and Sisulu from a nearby cell:

Mandela wethu/Our Mandela.
We will follow him.
Even if we are arrested, we will follow him.
Even if we are killed, we will follow him.

Sisulu wethu/Our Sisulu.
We will follow him.
Even if we are arrested, we will follow him.
Even if we are killed, we will follow him.

She sang almost the whole day. There may have been other songs, but that is the one that rang in my head.

She was like a whole chorus by herself. She didn't give a fuck. We were all in single cells, so the sound echoed even louder as it bounced off the walls of her cell and into each of ours. That she didn't try to communicate with us made her act of defiance even braver.

I've never met that woman who was so fearless and who gave us the strength to say, 'Go to hell.' Maybe they killed her. If I ever meet her, I will bow to her and say: 'You made my day when I was in a difficult situation. You raised my spirits and my courage.'

We male prisoners said to ourselves, 'If a woman can stand up and sing so loudly like this, who are we to be afraid?' So we sang a song about Azania, 'Home that I love'. And a lament that stated: 'This burden of freedom is too heavy. Tried and tested soldiers are needed to fight this war.' You would hear a male voice from another cell and start joining the song. It was also a song of intent. Soon, other songs started to be sung.

LATER, AS I WAS being beaten and interrogated, the woman's voice rang in my head. There were many courageous women like her in the struggle, who earned the title of 'tried and tested'. I don't know if she was a soldier, who she was, if she was in the student movement. You could hear that she was not old, just a young girl. But she knew what she was doing.

At meetings of ex-political prisoners, I always ask the women there if they know who she was or what happened to her, or if one of them was the one who was singing. 'We do not know who she was,' they tell me. 'She was not one of us.'

MY MOTHER WAS NOT happy when I was arrested after being in the forefront of the June 16 uprising in Alexandra because I was still of a tender age. But then she remembered the prophecy that had come to her before she was pregnant with me. 'This thing has gotten started now,' she told herself.

When I went to prison and later took up arms, it told her something definite. She didn't like it, but she understood what was happening.

I would not learn about that for many years, however.

You had to go to 'Number 4', the other name for the Old Fort Prison in Johannesburg, when you were arrested. Sometimes they beat me the whole night until the early hours of the morning to force me to sign a statement saying that I was attempting to overthrow the government. The district magistrate was supposed to be assisting me. Instead he was beating me, too. I decided that it was better to sign the confession and deny it in court so they didn't kill me. A court of law was the only place you could dispute an accusation's validity.

The trial took place from Monday to Friday over a two-week period. I was Accused Number 2. I was charged with high treason for furthering the aims of the ANC, which they labelled an unlawful organisation trying to overthrow the government. Two policemen used to pick me up in a Datsun Laurel every morning to accompany me to court. And almost every morning, there was a bomb blast somewhere in the city as the result of ANC activity.

That made things difficult for me, because this was what the authorities were responding to each day. They would give me the news in the morning. I didn't know what was going on because I was locked up.

'Do you know what your brothers did last night?' they would ask me when they came to pick me up. 'Who are my brothers?' I would reply. I did not know that the ANC were doing it in solidarity with other triallists and me. 'Thank you very much for supporting me,' I can now say.

After we arrived in court on the first day, the prosecutor opened the Bible and explained how they would charge me and why. It was a big, cold, unfriendly courtroom. The judge was a serious Afrikaner. But what they were doing was just a sham: I was sentenced before I even went through the court procedure.

The prosecutor called me a terrorist and recommended towards the end of the case that I be sentenced to 20 years or more. The officials took a break for lunch before the judge came back and set a day for my sentencing. (The court would be in session from the morning until 3 in the afternoon. We would adjourn for lunch and come back again.)

They invited a professor of political science, whose name I have forgotten, to testify. He droned on and on, talking about the history of the ANC and about the ANC's armed struggle. He also talked about all the bombings taking place, and it seemed clear that they wanted to link those to my trial.

The prosecutor quoted from the Bible on the day of the verdict, asserting that the other defendants and I had done the crimes we were accused of. 'These people committed a crime before God,' he said. We were aware that they had already convicted us in their minds before the trial even began. The only matter of interest to us at that point was finding out our sentences.

THEY EVEN PUT MY mother on the stand. 'This is a dangerous path,' she would tell me before I was arrested. 'Don't take it. Mandela is in jail. Your grandfather was involved in those things. Don't do it.' I was worried, to be honest, that she would side with these government guys.

She did not.

'What do you think about your son?' the authorities asked her gruffly. 'He is a terrorist who is trying to overthrow the government.'

Typically a person of a cheerful disposition, my mother was dead serious when she answered. 'He's not hurt anyone. He's not stolen from anyone. He's not raped anyone. He's fighting for what's right. I'm proud of him.'

The authorities removed her forcibly from the stand and I was sentenced to ten years in jail. Four of those years were suspended, however. I got six years in jail in the end.

They didn't give my mother or other relatives like my older sister a chance to hug me goodbye. They just sent me to the holding cells. My mother spoke to me as I walked down the stairs: 'Be strong. Don't break.'

The police came downstairs the day I left to serve my sentence, first at the Johannesburg prison called the Fort and then on Robben Island. 'You must greet Oliver Tambo for us,' they said, sliding a finger across their throat. 'How am I going to greet Oliver Tambo in jail? He's not in jail,' I answered. 'You must say hi to Mandela for us,' they replied. They were full of shit, those guys, but they were feeling confident at that moment.

When she came to visit me on Robben Island, my mother said to me, 'Why do you look like this? What have they been doing to you?'

'No, no! Don't say that,' I replied. 'It's you who are breaking me now.' Despite my words to her then, I didn't let that happen.

MY MOTHER DIED in 1990, while I was still in exile. That didn't break me, either, but it is still hard.

3
ROBBEN ISLAND

Immediately after the trial, my fellow political prisoners and I were taken back to the Old Fort and given our prison uniforms. We stayed in the prison for about two weeks. It was not a good place to be. You would meet gangsters in the reception area. We political prisoners were mostly isolated from the rest of the population, but you would see other prisoners being harassed or punished by gangs.

I remember the mornings when you got shaved. You would meet with the gangsters in the yard. Out of nowhere, they would hit you on the ear with an aluminium cup. They would also tie belts around the cups and hit each other on the head. This happened when you were lining up to have your hair cut, too. You would hide to avoid being hit. There were no politics at work here: it was a free zone. This meant that you could be affected even if you were not part of a gang and might be innocent of any real or imagined transgression. They were not fighting you, but you could become a casualty anyway. It was very intense and unpredictable.

The warders would take charge of the space after this 'battle of the gangs'. You would wait to have your hair cut, which was something other prisoners took care of. Haircutting did not take place in cells. You arrived during the day or at night, they processed you, and the next morning they cut your hair in the yard. They did an excellent job of it. After that, you were sent back to your cell for a couple of weeks.

The two guys who used to accompany me in the taxi were no longer at the Old Fort when I went back there after being sentenced. I had to travel in the same van as criminals who had robbed, raped and killed. This made me uncomfortable, but I received both a lesson and a pleasant surprise. They asked me why I'd been arrested, and I told them. When we reached the Fort, the criminals put out the order: 'Don't touch this one.'

It amazed me that criminals held liberation figures in high esteem and viewed political prisoners as freedom fighters. Young as I was – only fifteen years old – I was shown respect at prison reception. Later, when they came past the isolation cell in which I was being held, they would give me food when they could.

I was beginning to settle in when I was called and told that the authorities were transferring me to Leeuwkop Prison, a maximum-security prison in Bryanston. (I only learned recently that that's where it was.) They didn't tell us: they just took us there.

The transport guys came to take me to Leeuwkop on a Monday or a Tuesday. One of them, a white Afrikaner, was dressed casually in a t-shirt.

I heard a shout of 'Terrorist!' outside my cell. 'Terrorist?' I said aloud. 'Who are they calling?' It may have seemed that I was trying to make a political statement, but I honestly didn't know that the comment was aimed at me. A white prison warder opened the cell door and came in. I wouldn't be able to identify the guy today, and I certainly couldn't point him out in a line-up. But I do remember that he tried to get me suitably dressed.

'Don't dress like this,' he was saying. 'Terrorists don't dress like this.' He tucked my shirt inside my trousers without asking for my permission. 'Now let's go,' he ordered. It felt pretty intimidating, but I guess he just wanted me to look good.

You were transferred to an isolation cell when you got to Leeuwkop Prison. You would only meet other prisoners at the hospital. They also would give you their respect when they found out who you were. If you were there for rape, you were in for shit. But if they found out that you were there for advancing the aims of the ANC, you would pass because 'you are fighting for us'.

There was a guy in our section at Leeuwkop who was there for bank robberies and for selling marijuana. He was said to have been sentenced to between 60 and 90 years. Nobody seemed to know the length for sure, but it was one of those endless sentences. He had earned himself the title of 'godfather of the mafias', and in Soweto he had been known by his nickname of 'UmCaravan'. His real name was Sipho Sibeko, and we called him 'Bra Sipho'.

Bra Sipho was a humble person, by no means the arrogant man his title may have suggested. He was two cells away from me and would come to his cell door at two in the morning to ask me if I was all right. Clean-living and religious, he was a different kind of character from the usual criminal.

He prayed every morning and sang church songs every night. He would pray for hours, asking for forgiveness for what he had done on the outside. He also used to sing an isiXhosa hymn that still resonates with me today: 'Bawo Ndixolele. Father, the Creator, please forgive what I have done. Forgive me for all my sins.'

Bra Sipho also negotiated on our behalf with the authorities. He helped organise for everybody to be allowed together in the same cell on weekends, when we would play Monopoly. We would often be discussing Marxism–Leninism while we were playing Monopoly and buying hotels. Scrabble was another game that was popular with us.

FROM LEEUWKOP PRISON, we were sent on to Robben Island, off the coast of Cape Town. We made the journey in a prison truck. The armed guards would stop once in a while, open the prison truck and let us relieve ourselves one by one. We had a tin at the back of the truck that we would shit into after we ate. All of us were handcuffed and wore chains on our legs.

Our first stop was Bloemfontein Prison, because the guards wanted to be able to relieve themselves in the staff toilets there. The Afrikaner warders shouted at us before they let us out to use the prisoners' amenities: 'Don't talk! There's no noise allowed.'

There was a guy with us who was from the Witbank area and whose name was Johannes Shabangu. He walked down the metal steps leading out of the truck, holding his chains. He threw them down as he got to the last step. They landed with a deafening clattering noise.

Of course, it could have been unintentional. But it wasn't, and he started calling us by name. 'Hey, Khulu,' he said to me loudly.

That was defiance. After I'd lifted and dropped my chains, David Moisi, another prisoner, did the same, and it was on. We began to chant as we went through the prison entrance and down the prison corridor leading to the toilets that were intended for inmates. We were chanting just to break the law.

We went back to the truck after we'd gone to the toilet, still chanting loudly. The warders couldn't do anything about our behaviour. They were already taking us to prison, and they couldn't punish all of us.

We repeated the cycle in Worcester. Park the truck. Off to the toilet. More noise and defiance. Finally, at about 3 am, we reached the last stop, which was at the waterfront near the docks.

We were chatting and talking in the truck, but it wasn't as if we were having a good time. We were intensely aware that we were going to jail. They put us in a holding cell for the rest of the night after we arrived.

In the morning, they brought a boat to take us over to the island. It was misty on the docks when they placed us in the hold. Now positioned above us, they took their revenge by peeing on us.

That was the price they made us pay for our small moments of rebellion. We were in chains when they urinated on us. I'd never envisaged that such a thing was possible when I'd set off on that journey from Leeuwkop. We were on a boat that already smells terrible and we're underneath, in the hold, where the stench is strongest. And these motherfuckers are peeing on us, while saying 'Kom, kom, kom' as if they are calling dogs. It was intolerable to see some of the older prisoners humiliated in this way.

WE COULDN'T DO anything at that moment, but there was war when we arrived on Robben Island and they took us off the boat. We started grabbing and hitting them when they removed our chains. We fought those people hard.

They overpowered us and took us to the prison reception, and then to the isolation cells. We knew where we were going and we didn't care. We knew that we were finished if we gave in at that point. We had to take a stand right there.

I fought until I left the Island.

I WAS NERVOUS BEFORE I got to Robben Island. Although we had all been sentenced as political prisoners, I did not know all these other people. I didn't have any idea how I would relate to them. The funny thing is that I need not have worried. As I soon found out, they were welcoming and had a high level of consciousness.

At the beginning I tried to hold back – to hold on to myself. They attempted to engage with me, but I was guarded at first because I knew certain stories about prisons. I'd heard that some older guys wanted to abuse you sexually. I soon realised something important about those people. They never abused anyone, not in a single cell. The ANC guys didn't do that, anyway.

The older ANC guys did not rape the younger prisoners, but the Xhosa men among them circumcised the younger Xhosa guys. They would find a razor somehow and circumcise them. The young men would always heal. One of my comrades was circumcised in jail, if I'm not mistaken. While it would happen one at a time, a whole group of people was responsible for carrying out the rite of passage in the best possible way.

It was a sacred ritual, which on Robben Island would take place at the toilets. They would chase you away when you came close to the toilets. Those who were circumcised would continue with a certain educational course on how to become a man in the Xhosa tradition.

We had people on the island from Johannesburg, from the length and the breadth of South Africa and Namibia. IsiXhosa, not IsiZulu, was the dominant language on the island. I didn't know isiXhosa before I went into jail and I learned it there.

I WAS CALLED TO the Administration Office for an interview with the head of prisons in South Africa shortly after arriving on Robben

Island. He was like a Director General of prisons. His team was there, too. The purpose of the interview was to determine which section of the prison they were going to put you. They would categorise you as a more or less dangerous person based on your answers.

The head had powers to place the prisoners in any section.

He was a strong Afrikaner guy, middle-aged with a moustache. He had well-organised hair and was wearing a prison warder's jersey.

He was polite, with a gentle demeanour. His way was to try to get prisoners to open up. Civilised and educated, he would offer them tea, cake and a cigarette.

When he asked me if I wanted some tea, I said, 'No, I'm fine.' How could I trust these guys?

'Do you want some cigarettes?' someone else on his team wondered. I explained that I did not smoke.

I was also told, 'We are just friends here. You are reacting as if we are in a conflict situation.'

'I'm okay,' I answered. 'Let's talk.'

They started asking me questions that took place over the course of two long days. We spoke in English the whole time.

'Are you a member of the Communist Party?' they asked. 'Are you a member of the student movement?'

'No,' I replied every time.

'Then what is your take on the South African situation?' they asked me. 'What type of South Africa do you think you want? How should South Africa be?'

We started debating at this point.

I said that I would love to see a South Africa where all of us lived in peace and harmony, a land where there was no bloodshed. We should own the factories together, we should own the wealth of this country. (At that time, I did not know the phrase 'means of production'.) We should also break with the practice of segregation in all things, I proposed.

They listened to me as I argued with the head, who had a big voice when he got going. I didn't quarrel with them. I just debated in a peaceful way, as if we were having a discussion.

'Thank you very much, Mr Radebe, for meeting with us,' they

said at the end of the first day. 'It was a pleasure talking with you. We hope we meet again.' Polite and respectful.

I was surprised when I realised that I might be further charged for the positions I was advancing. I had been unaware of that possibility when I started the debate. You didn't know what their intentions were. But I took a decision: 'Who cares? I'm here already. If they sentence me further, what do I have to be scared of?'

Fortunately, while they could have charged me for my statements, they didn't do so.

Their view of me had changed, though. 'Get out,' they told me at the end of the second day. 'You're a communist.'

'No, I'm not a communist. I don't even remember their code.'

'That *is* who you are,' was their reply. I could see that the head of prisons had categorised me as a terrorist.

They put me in the F Section, along with the most rule-breaking and notorious prisoners.

YOU UNDERWENT OBSERVATION at the hospital for a couple of weeks before being transferred to your cell. No more isolation. The cell you ended up in depended on what you had said during your interviews. That falsely friendly man determined what happened: 'Don't put him in this section. Put him in that section.' You also started engaging with the *bou span*, the building team who carried out physical work.

While all of this was going on, the political leaders were checking you inside and out to assess whether you were a genuine comrade. It took you six months to integrate into the community on Robben Island. You didn't fit in right away. The ordinary prisoners asked you for news from outside, from the area you came from. They might want to know whether somebody from the township was still alive. They were genuinely friendly and treating you normally, but they did not open up about politics. They were talking about topics like sports 'under G' (the category called 'General'), and that was it. They also played sports with you.

They didn't talk about sensitive topics with you. They wanted to make sure that you were not being planted on them by the enemy. You were settling in, observing, making friends. Until you had proved yourself otherwise, they basically took you for one of those young boys who were full of shit.

AFTER THAT PERIOD of six months, which is what it took to properly verify and clear you, they would come to you and say: 'Your course is starting. From now on, you will be getting the scoop.'

There were many among those on the island who were planted. The Afrikaners would send in a black guy who would act as a spy for them. Luckily, the leaders could often find out from their lawyers if someone was planted.

Many lawyers, especially those acting on behalf of senior struggle prisoners, were in political sympathy with their clients. As a result, they were able to tap into underground information networks capable of checking the truthfulness of the claims new prisoners might make about their past. Or comrades on the outside might approach the lawyers to relay information to their clients during their permitted confidential visits. 'This one has been planted,' the lawyers would say.

The spies would be isolated after being detected. As soon as the leadership found out what their game was, everyone was immediately warned against them. If they came along to sit with us when we were sitting together, we would stand up and walk away. And if they tried to talk to individuals among us, these people would refuse and move away.

The capacity of the prison authorities to pin further charges on us was one of the reasons we chose avoidance and silence. They would set up a tribunal and appoint their own prosecutor. This could add years to your sentence. Mine could easily have grown from six years to twelve years, for example. They would judge you harshly. They'd sentence you and you'd be finished. You'd end up dying in jail. That's why you had to stay away from spies. It was easy to imagine your sentence growing and growing, and your family being left bereft when you failed to return.

We regularly took part in constructive criticism sessions. The criticism was based on your political background, your knowledge, your education. Constructive criticism would enable you to know the difference between right and wrong.

You didn't begin with constructive criticism. You had to start with the history of South Africa before the colonisers arrived, and then go through the history of South Africa under colonialism. From there you'd learn about Karl Marx and Friedrich Engels, and also about Marxism–Leninism. After that you would be taught the history of the ANC and the Pan Africanist Congress (PAC). When you'd graduated from that level, you'd have to be armed with the tools of analysis for international politics, so that you could make use of constructive criticism on a wider platform at a later stage.

We arrived in jail as young, vibrant, hot-tempered people. This process turned us into mature youths. Developing the proper political background (we used to call it the 'tools of analysis') gave you more information and made you better equipped for the struggle.

You also never criticised a person without providing solutions to build that person up. That was the constructive part – it came from an informed point of view. When you were being criticised, you were meant to understand that you *were* wrong. You did not need to be criticised often, because you had the knowledge you needed to distinguish between right and wrong.

There were two types of constructive criticism. One-on-one constructive criticism was known as 'a taxi', while a session that involved a group meeting was called 'a bus'.

I quickly learned on Robben Island that jokes are political. Before passing a joke in the presence of another person, you must first weigh the disadvantages and advantages of that specific joke in that specific context. You must look at the content of the joke, and evaluate how it is going to affect the person involved.

That's how critical we were in jail. We applied the principle of weighing up the impact of our actions in everything we did.

I'll never forget a Saturday afternoon on which a certain guy made a joke aimed at another prisoner. 'Do not behave like Matanzima,' he said. Kaiser Matanzima was the leader, in the Eastern Cape, of one of the black bantustans or homelands.

'Why do you categorise me with sellouts?' the guy on the receiving end of the joke replied. The situation quickly escalated as he started asking other prisoners: 'I understand that he says it's a joke. But is he saying that I'm a sellout? That's what I'm trying to understand.' The tension was running higher and higher and it was soon clear that the two were aiming for a fight. The man who felt he'd been insulted made some angry comments. But the other man surprised us by choosing not to retaliate and to defuse the angry situation instead.

'Why were you quiet when he was saying those things to you?' we asked him afterward.

'You know why I was quiet?' he replied. 'This man showed that his level of comprehension is low. He didn't understand the point I was making. I can't fight with him now, because I have a long journey ahead with him.'

'What long journey?' we wanted to know.

'We are fighting against apartheid,' he responded. 'It will be a long fight and I need him on this journey. If I fight him now, I'll lose him. I need him to stay on board. So what I'm going to do is wait for him to calm down. Even though he is wrong, I'm going to go to him tomorrow and submit as if I'm the one who was wrong. This will show him that I still need him. My call is to have him on my side, so that we both continue fighting the enemy. One day, he will realise that he was wrong. Proving that to him now is not my call.'

We learned from guys like that.

OUR FIGHTS TOOK many forms, and they were not always among ourselves. One example was the solitary fight Sipho Ngcobo waged against the warders.

A PAC member, Sipho was quiet and a former journalist. (When he came back to South Africa in the 1990s, he worked at *The Star* newspaper.) He ate everything on his plate, half a spoon at a time, ponderously chewing every bite and frustrating the prison warders who wanted to close the cells for the night. Based on the regulations, they had to wait for Sipho to finish his plate. You could see how frustrated they were, folding their arms across their chests as they waited for him to finish his food.

He was doing this on purpose, of course.

'Why do you do this?' we asked him.

'I'm fighting my war with these guys. They will have to wait for me. I don't care if their shift is done, they will wait until I'm finished eating.'

They waited. They expected to close the doors at about four in the afternoon. But with Sipho around, they left between half past five or six.

I LEARNED A LOT about housework and cleanliness while I was on Robben Island. I had done a fair amount of chores at home, but the need to keep things under control intensified in prison because I was always kept in the isolation cells before being put in Section F.

This meant, for one thing, that I had to prepare my blankets myself. There was an inspection every morning, during which the warders would be looking for reasons to complain. So you had to be a model of tidiness and cleanliness. I kept up those practices when I went into exile.

Another reason I learned to be clean was that I had competition from clean old men like Govan Mbeki – who we called 'Oom Gov' or 'Uncle Gov' – and Nelson Mandela. There were other older prisoners there – guys like Sandy Lebese and Henry Fazzie, a comrade we used to call 'Tata Fazzie' – who were not as well known as those two but were just as neat and orderly. I used to hang around a lot with them and liked to emulate them. We younger prisoners learned a lot from them just by observing.

Govan Mbeki gave me a lecture one day some years after I arrived on the island. I was playing tennis, and was wearing my tennis shorts, a t-shirt and some white socks. Oom Gov sent somebody to call me. I thought there was an emergency. It turned out he had summoned me because my t-shirt was outside my shorts.

He began to lecture me. 'Why do you have to put your t-shirt outside your shorts?' he asked. He spoke slowly and with authority. He had been a teacher by profession. His lecture went on. Not for 20 minutes, not for 60 minutes, but *days*.

Leaders of the ANC and the South African Communist Party (SACP) supported the principles that Oom Gov expounded during his lectures. 'When you walk in the street, you must walk the walk of the liberation movement,' he said. 'People must be inspired. They must wish to be part of your life.' He went on, 'Even if you're wearing a jacket or a coat, people must say, "Wow, that's a Congress man walking here."'

He gave other examples too: how Lenin used to dress, how other leaders like Georgi Dimitrov handled themselves. His advice was wide-ranging: 'Don't sleep around with girlfriends, don't hang around with the wrong people, and don't do wrong things in society because that will impact on you. Every day of your life, you write a chapter of your book. One day, you'll want to feel that you are somebody in your society. It will be then that people will refer to that book.'

This was what Oom Gov did when he pulled me off the tennis court, on that day and on many days after that. He was well aware that I could never finish the game I had started. The next morning he called me off the court again because he hadn't finished sharing his beliefs with me. This was the case even on Saturdays and Sundays.

He was outstanding at indoctrination. Whenever he spoke to you, you'd feel that something had been removed from your brain and that your prior way of thinking had changed. 'Wow, *this* is how things are supposed to be,' I'd say to myself after each session.

I grew a lot on Robben Island, which was more like an initiation period than a prison term for me. In addition to changing my clothing style, I also started to carry myself differently.

Part of the education on the island entailed being politically conscientised about sex.

We were taught that sex was not important on the island and that we should not worry about making love. We were also taught the philosophy of love. They told us, 'If you leave prison and you want to get married, these are the phases that you need to undertake so that you don't make mistakes.'

THE FIRST PHASE COVERS meeting a woman that you like and want to create a friendship with. You introduce yourself, after which she introduces herself. From there you make an appointment, like a date, for you to meet.

If you agree to meet, you move to the second phase. That is when you meet in a restaurant or in a park, or wherever you're going to sit down and talk. The two of you.

The second phase is the most crucial phase of your life, the one that determines your future, how you're going to end up in your life. You sit down with this woman and you talk about your own family background. After you have done this, she talks about her family background. She talks about things she doesn't like and things she likes. You do the same.

If there is an understanding, you move to the third phase. You then say, 'Okay, I think I will assist you if you have problems.' She'll say the same thing. So you agree to work together in trying to deal with obstacles. As you do this, you assess whether you are reaching the desired mutual agreement, partnership or relationship. You agree to have fortnightly constructive criticism meetings. This is just between the two of you.

You review what is happening, meet and talk about the obstacles you said you would be working on together so as to build a better relationship. You assist each other.

That fortnightly constructive meeting continues until you die. You observe that even when you are old, because applying it brings down the level of miscommunication and argument.

You agree not to argue in front of your kids, you don't argue in front of any other people. Instead, you tell each other, 'If you have issues about wrong things that you have done, we'll park it for a fortnight and deal with it as fast as possible within that time frame.'

The fourth phase is when you know that you understand each other well. You are now 'going out' and are ready to be introduced to your prospective in-laws. Only then do they come in. Once you have done that, you move to a fifth phase during which you are actively planning to get married.

No sex is involved this entire time. That doesn't happen until you get married, until you say: '*Now* we know each other. We understand each other's weak and strong characteristics, we can tolerate each other's tempers, we can be husband and wife.'

Why did we learn this? They told us that if you applied those phases and that philosophy of love, it would help you to avoid situations where a woman felt or said, 'That guy never liked me, that guy abused me. He just wanted to meet me for sex; and that's it.' It eliminates that.

You never want to fall into a trap with a lot of women telling you accusingly: 'You slept with me, you did this to me. You used me.' They reminded us that 'Tomorrow you're going to be a leader, you don't need to have those obstacles in your life.'

That's what we were taught in jail.

The University of Makana on Robben Island had what may be referred to as a broad curriculum that offered a wide variety of subjects. The university was named after a courageous Xhosa prophet and king who had resisted land grabs by British colonial forces and whom the British had imprisoned on the island in 1819. He had drowned in an attempt to escape from it.

We discussed many topics at the University of Makana. Moreover, there was a real system to the education we received on the island.

You not only resisted apartheid every second of the day while preparing for the future. If the High Command decided that you needed to take a certain course that would be helpful in preparing you for the role you would later play in a free country, they would make sure that the one who was teaching that subject went to you. 'Khulu needs to learn Marxism and Leninism,' they would say. The best teacher for the job would find you and hang out with you.

There was also a policy that determined your progress through the university. They moved at your pace, based on how you were grasping the material. When the lecturer finished discussing the topic, he would review the work and make sure you had understood it. The next day, they would assess how much you had understood and pick up from the point where you had forgotten. If you'd mastered the material, he moved away from you and attended to another prisoner.

They were unusually patient, as they had to make sure that you would remember what you had been taught when you got out of prison and carried out your assigned task.

It was constant education by the same prisoners who had been professionals before being imprisoned. Some of them were teachers, others were doctors, and yet others had been lawyers.

The prison authorities may have realised that education was taking place on the island, but our young Afrikaner guards had no idea – no idea at all – of the talent that was gathered there. Most interested in making their professional mark, they had no sense of prisoners as individuals with varied professional backgrounds. Their ignorance and racial prejudice worked to our advantage in this respect, offsetting the fact that we were forever being spied on.

Thembinkosi Sithole, a tall guy from Durban who cherished Marxism and Leninism, used to love talking about how the arts developed. We would talk often during the long hours of the many hunger strikes we took part in.

He believed that sex had played an important role in language development. The point when someone reached orgasm and started just saying things was one of the ways language had begun, he said. People who were angry and expressed their feelings through sounds had also contributed to language development. But the arts, started in early times by people who could craft stone, preceded language. The animals that were crafted onto rock had also contributed to the development of language, he believed. 'What was their inner reflection? What was it they were thinking?' he would ask himself and anyone listening to him.

Language, he said, had made communication possible between people who lived high on a mountain, next to a waterfall, and those who lived down below, at the foot of the waterfall. He asked himself questions about the nature of that communication and came to certain conclusions. Large distances explained why you found people in different regions of the world who spoke loudly, as many Nigerians did. They spoke loudly because of the problems caused by distance, and their way of speaking had become the norm. They still spoke loudly even though Lagos was so crowded and people lived in such close proximity.

Thembinkosi also believed that language and the arts had developed together, and that the inner part of a person is expressed through their soul and through the arts. He spoke about music, drawing and dance. He explained that the origin of Zulu dances was an expression of – or a reflection on – what a man felt about the cattle he owned. The man who was performing the dance would use his hands to mimic the shape and movement of each of his animals' horns. He would move in a different way for the first cow, the second cow, the third cow, and so on.

This is not something everyone knows about. That's what I mean when I say that the island was a university. We really learned a lot there.

PART OF MY EDUCATION was learning what *not* to ask. One day, soon after I arrived, I asked aloud, 'What time is it?'

Everybody responded with a single word: 'What?!'

'I just want to know what time it is,' I repeated.

'What are you going to do with the time?' they answered.

Someone decided to explain: 'No prisoner asks for the time. You're the only one saying, What time is it? When the prison warder locks you up, you know you have shortened your sentence that day. You also know that a new day is coming. That's all that matters.' Someone else advised: 'Don't ask that here. You'll go crazy if you keep asking what time it is. Just go on. When you're called to be told you're being released, that's when you'll need to know what the time is.'

So I didn't ask again.

It was very cold on the island, which is surrounded by the Atlantic Ocean. It was often below freezing. I pity the slaves who were taken across the ocean without proper clothing. That is one reason why many of them died.

The warders used to wake us up in the early hours of the morning. 'Strip search,' they would say. They would usually wait for an exceptionally cold day when it was also raining. Then they would make us stand naked outside and pour freezing water over us.

We would stand there for hours while they were checking everything in the cell. They said that they were looking for banned material, including banned literature. They used this procedure when searching for knives or other dangerous weapons in the criminal section. People who carried sharp objects, handmade knives or spoons inevitably came from the criminal side. We were political prisoners – not that they ever called us that. They labelled us 'security prisoners'.

Many people developed chest problems and asthma as a result of the damp floors during these searches. To me, it was just harassment. If they found something, you'd be charged again. They would open a new case against you and you would get a further sentence. You would be put through a trial on the island or on the mainland, depending on how serious the charge was.

Sometimes guys would get caught with banned material, usually part of the secret teaching materials and methods developed for education on the island. Teachers would usually write on the ground; or they would talk to you quietly while moving at your pace. There was also a system whereby you could be taught through notes written on toilet paper. Teachers might cover Marxist and Leninist concepts, like the history of dialectical and historical materialism, on toilet paper, for example. You'd read through them before using the toilet paper for its intended purpose. We were taught an art of remembering so that you wouldn't carry anything incriminating on you.

The guards would be frustrated when they didn't find anything and would come in with their hosepipes. They would pour water on our blankets and on our clothes, and drench everything in our cells. 'You're a fucking …,' they would swear at us as they were doing it.

They were trying to break us so that when we got off the island we wouldn't partake in any political activities.

It was very heavy to deal with, but we just kept quiet at first.

WE DID TALK ABOUT these experiences with Nelson Mandela, who was the head of our committee. He and the other leaders in the Makhulu Span (team), or 'Senior Group', were on their own in B Section, which had the most privileges. They helped us whenever we had to deal with issues of school bursaries, school books, or whatever other nitty-gritty matters we were trying to sort out. They would, in effect, negotiate for us. We would even send grievances against the authorities to the committee. They were our voice in such interactions. Around 1983, the authorities adopted a policy that said prisoners from different sections could not meet with each other. I don't know why they did this. It appeared to be an attempt to separate us from each other. Prisoners who came to the island after our release told us that the policy didn't work and the authorities abandoned it in 1984 or 1985.

We started by engaging with Mandela, Govan Mbeki and the Makhulu Span about the strip searches, and they assured us that they were already handling the matter.

'But you are not handling it,' we replied. 'You're not handling it in the right way, because the harassment is continuing. The other issues – around school – are fine.'

'No, listen, young guys, comrades. We *are* talking to them,' they answered. 'We'll find a solution to these problems.'

We younger prisoners trusted the members of the Makhulu Span. But we young boys who were in cell block F were so unhappy about the strip searches that we came to a firm conclusion and took a decision: 'You know what? If we don't stop this nonsense now, no one is going to stop it. These older ones are being crazy. They will say something to the officials again, but nothing will change. Let's embark on a hunger strike. Let's start fighting.'

NORMALLY, IT WAS THE Makhulu Span from B Section who called a hunger strike. Everything was done through the upper structures. There were also structures responsible for sports and politics, and everything was properly coordinated in a collective manner. This time, we told the Makhulu Span that we were fed up. They could go on eating. We were going on strike.

We had taken this decision in the communal section after several months of waiting for change. Even there I was not in control – I was just one of the fighters. We mobilised the whole prison, starting with F Section. Then it was D Section, E Section, then C. When it came to B Section, we compromised: 'They must eat because they're old, they've got medical conditions,' we said.

The strike went on for more than a month. We refused to work since we were not eating and just stayed in our cells. We were not going anywhere… The warders thought we were crazy. They didn't know that the secret of the hunger strike's success lay in our anger. Nothing will make you eat when you are angry. When somebody gives you food, you say, 'No, I am fine.' We were angry and bitter, and had made our decision, once and for all, not to eat.

The guards would put food out in front of us and offer it to us. They would bring chicken straight to your cell on weekends. They would braai it in the kitchen and bring it to you. The smells. Wow! Yet we were never tempted, because we knew why we were fighting. Instead, we told them that we did not want their cooks in the kitchen anymore; and that in future we would want only our own guys to do the cooking. This was the latest in a long list of demands that went well beyond the call for an end to strip searches.

We demanded that they stop harassing us and listen to our grievances. We told them that we wanted sports privileges. Most of the guys who were grounded in D group had not advanced far in their schooling and needed to go ahead with their education. We in F Section also wanted to go to school.

Some of the guys collapsed while we were on hunger strike, and the authorities would try to give them a glucose drip for energy. They refused. 'If Oliver Tambo tells me to accept the drip, I will do it,' they would say. 'If that order comes from Lusaka, I will do it. Don't bring the order verbally. It must be written and signed by Tambo. Then I will do it. Otherwise, no.' They were truly the 'tried and tested' participants of that strike.

Our struggle led to a victory. In the end the authorities stopped the strip searches and agreed to all of our demands. We gained privileges for sports like tennis. We had asked to access books we chose ourselves at the prison library. That was agreed to as well. Finally, they gave us enough encyclopaedias to fill a barge.

THE AUTHORITIES REGARDED Thembinkosi – he of the language development theories – and me as the two prisoners who were most full of shit. In late 1983, they planned something for us by pretending that they were taking us to a hospital. Just the two of us.

This was under the pretext that the doctor had to give us a check-up.

The doctor was known as Pesco. I don't know why we called him that. I do know that he was not a qualified doctor. We used to say he was a donkey because he was an animal doctor. He would give you a paracetamol no matter what you were sick with. A certain prisoner who was sick with a stomach ulcer and rolling on the floor from pain was admitted to hospital. Pesco still just gave the prisoner paracetamol – and he died.

Pesco and the authorities connived to send us for a check-up, and took us off the island to Groote Schuur Hospital instead. On the way back from the hospital, we realised that they were not taking us back to the island. They were taking us somewhere to try to break us.

We took a long journey to the town of Caledon in the Cape. Our destination was Helderstroom Prison. We soon saw that it was practically empty of prisoners despite being a large institution. We were the only two in the section we entered. There may have been other people in another section.

It was obvious they were isolating us. They put us in different cells, me in the first cell and Thembinkosi a number of cells away. We were not supposed to be able to talk to each other, but we did – loudly.

We took the decision to go on a hunger strike the instant we walked in and understood their plan. 'We are not going to stay here, man. The best thing is for us to embark on a hunger strike. Right now. We're not going to eat anything from these guys. Let's hold on to the plates. They give us food, we kick it over. They give us something to drink, even tea, we kick it to the floor. Anything. We just kick everything,' Thembinkosi declared.

The people who cooked for us were what we call common-law prisoners. I remember them bringing us things like carrot balls. Whenever they brought us food, we just kicked it away. This went on for a couple of weeks, maybe even a month.

Helderstroom Prison was extremely cold. Our cells were the normal unheated isolation cells with bare walls. There was no bed, just a mat. You had some blankets for when you went to sleep and a bucket in which to relieve yourself. That was it.

The warders tried to neutralise us by bringing in prisoners who were 'on exit', which meant that they had just one or two months left of their sentences. 'I'm gonna do this, I'm gonna do that,' they'd be saying while you had at least three years left of your sentence. This was the kind of torture they subjected us to. But they didn't break us.

They also brought in Hunter, a guard who wanted to be my friend. Slender and old, he was a serious-looking lieutenant with two stars who had guarded Mandela. He was also a smoker who tried to convince me to behave. 'I worked with Mandela and never had issues,' he would tell me. I didn't care what he said.

Hunter would tell us, 'Don't worry, I'm here,' as though he had the power to protect us. 'Nope, there's no Hunter here,' we replied to give him the lie. 'We don't care. We *want* to live here.'

We used to break our strike for a little while, just to stay alive, and then start again the next month.

At long last, they took us out of our cells and tried to tempt us: 'We want to bring your mother here. This is the best prison. We want you to realise that if you cooperate, we will take care of you. It's not like the island; you will have all the privileges that are granted to prisoners here. Don't worry.'

'No, go to hell,' we told them. 'We *want* to go back to the island. We want to be back with the other prisoners who have the same sentences as us.'

They persisted.

'Okay, a compromise. We'll be taking you to Pollsmoor with Mandela.'

'We don't want to be with Mandela.'

'But it will be a good thing.'

'Who says it will be a good thing? We don't want to be with him. Take us back to where you took us from,' I replied.

We didn't want to be separated from our comrades and so went back on the hunger strike. They had not understood who they were dealing with or the depth of our commitment.

Finally, the warders said, 'Okay, we'll see where you guys are going to go next.'

THE OTHER PRISONERS saluted us when we arrived back at the island because we had not given in.

The island authorities made us appear before them. 'If you strike again, we will never again allow you outside,' they threatened.

'Who cares, man?' I replied. 'We have what we want.'

THE AUTHORITIES CAME to fetch me one day when I was playing tennis. 'You have a visitor,' they told me.

'I don't want visitors,' I responded categorically.

Then Hunter appeared to tell me about my visitor. We spoke in Afrikaans.

'You have a visitor.'

'I don't want visitors when I'm working. Don't you see I'm playing a game?'

'It's your fucking mother, man. She is waiting for you.'

'Don't joke, man.'

'I'm serious, man. You think I can come here and joke? Come, man! Stop playing, man. I don't have time for playing.'

THAT WAS THE ONLY time my mother visited me when I was on Robben Island. The Red Cross had arranged a visit for her. They'd come to the house in Alex and told her about it. The visit only lasted 35 minutes.

She started crying when I appeared.

'Please, Mom,' I said. 'Don't. Don't. Don't.' I knew that if she kept crying, I would never be able to stop crying when she left.

'What did they do to you?'

'No. Don't ask. Please, please.'

We started our conversation in isiZulu and isiXhosa before a guard warned us: 'Speak English or speak Afrikaans. This man is going to listen to you. If you speak about things you shouldn't talk about, we can't allow the visit. We warn you first, then we cut short the visit.'

The man listening to us was an isiXhosa speaker who would also listen to the conversations between prisoners. He would stand there for hours. 'If he comes, change the topic,' I'd been told. 'Don't talk about politics because he'll open a new charge against you. That is his only work on the island.'

We used to call him 'Adjudant' (the Afrikaans for 'adjutant'). I've asked other ex-prisoners about him, and they don't remember his real name, either.

My mother told me to be strong and assured me she was holding her own. 'Don't worry. I'm strong,' she said. 'But you look different now.'

'No, don't worry about me,' I repeated before asking about everyone at home. We spent the rest of the time talking about what was happening in the family.

The visit ended with my telling her, 'Don't come again.'

HERS WAS THE ONLY visit I had the whole time I was there. I didn't want visitors because the guards could hold me hostage through them, and I didn't want to get into those battles because I wanted to concentrate on the struggle. I was also still young. Visitors mean nothing to you at that stage of life. Letters are not important, either. Those visits and correspondence might even pose a danger to the struggle if the warders successfully used them against me.

I wasn't worried about not having visits, but some of the guys who were older than me had never had a visit or even a letter. Some of them were in their sixties and felt that they had been abandoned by their families. In many cases, families *would* disown political prisoners. You would see that they were losing their spirit. Their morale would go down visibly, and we would say: 'They are being eaten by prison.' Sometimes, one of them acted as if mentally disturbed. The best thing to restore him was to get him a girlfriend on the outside. He would improve after that.

Some of the prisoners had not seen a woman for ten to fifteen years, except for a white lady who would bring us medicine. Sometimes you'd see women, maybe warders' wives or daughters, from a distance when you were driving past them in a prison truck. That was it. You would only see them. You could not engage them one-on-one.

When you went to Groote Schuur Hospital for a check-up, however, the woman radiographer would touch your body during the radiography exam and reassure you that nothing was going to hurt. You would talk about it with the other prisoners when you returned to the island. They would want to know all the details of what it was like and what you had felt. We used to call this experience 'isiManziso', which meant 'amazement'.

The leaders would organise a visit for each of the demoralised prisoners if at all possible. This would happen through the International Red Cross or the South African Council of Churches. The Council kept a database for many years of all the people who were in detention.

Most visits entailed great effort, and winning those battles meant a lot to us. Comrades on the outside would arrange for their female friends or family members to apply for a visitor spot or to write letters and send photos. A visit preceded or followed by correspondence was the best. Still, any personal contact made a substantial difference.

Some of the women who played a role in this were involved in the struggle in the urban areas. Others were women in rural areas who had become conscientised and were willing to keep the prisoner energised so he did not become cut-off and demoralised. When the guy got out of prison after being released, the woman he had been writing to might become his girlfriend. Some of these relationships lasted while others did not.

ONE INCIDENT OF rebellion I will never forget, and which I know is hard for almost anyone to believe, took place in the early morning as we were falling into groups to go to work. It was cloudy, as it nearly always is on the island at that time of day. I was in my usual team, the *bou span*.

I was already using a pick and shovel to break up sandy ground in the garden area and throwing the sand into wheelbarrows. This was a common job for our team. Sometimes I would also push a full wheelbarrow or two to the spot where I knew the sand would be needed.

Our team would then normally shift its efforts to the stone quarry at the back of the prison, where we would spend the day breaking larger stones into specified sizes. We were now ready to move along, and the teams that would be working in the garden were all waiting to get to work.

I was the first in my section. Suddenly, the man who was head of Robben Island at that time was standing in front of me. He had big shoulders and was full of shit. He was a bully, that bastard.

'Why are you looking at me?' he said to me.

'No, I'm very sorry,' I replied. 'I was not looking at you. It may have happened that I looked in your direction, but I'm sorry if you thought I was looking at you.' (The warders didn't like it if you looked directly at them and inevitably took it as confrontation.)

'Kak,' he told me, meaning that I was talking shit and that I *had* been looking at him.

'I'm apologising to you with respect, sir. I'm saying that if I looked in your direction, I was not looking at you directly, I'm sorry for that.'

'No, fuck you, man.'

'Are you wanting to confront me? I'm going to confront you back,' I heard myself answer.

Little did I realise that a time-bomb involving the rest of the prisoners was about to detonate. I had not been aware that the PAC and BC guys had a big grievance against this warder. They had not known how to initiate their protest, but they were ready for one. The guys from F Section also had an issue with him. So did the guys from E Section and the guys from D Section.

Despite being very angry, everyone was unsure how to start this thing. They were all watching me to see how I would react. They knew my attitude and knew that I was a fighter.

My anger was boiling up, but I kept quiet. 'Why do you insult me when I'm saying I'm sorry?' I asked.

'No, fuck you.'

'You know what? Fuck *you*, man.'

I started grabbing the bastard by the shirt. He was about the same height as me.

'I will hit you,' I promised him.

Without a second's pause, I hit him straight on the nose and he started to bleed. I knocked him down to the ground and the scene exploded. The prisoners all started to attack the warders. Complete chaos followed in the prison for a long time.

It had not been my intention to start a riot, but we fought

and fought once it began. The prisoners had been waiting for this moment. There was one BC guy from Limpopo who, I think, had been sentenced to seven years. He took off his prison clothes and demanded his civilian clothes.

We fought the whole day and a second day. The authorities started negotiating on the third day, and all the prisoners backed me.

'Khulu said sorry,' they stated to a man. 'Khulu has explained what happened. We were right next to him.'

The authorities could not charge me because of the prisoners' unwavering support, but I didn't avoid *all* consequences. As was to be expected, the head of prisons was incredibly angry and tried to find fault with everything I did. Prior to that I had only been aware of him from a distance. Our battle had bound us together in a close hatred. I became his worst enemy and he started watching my every move.

It was around that time that they started a type of punishment with the name of *drie maal*. They locked you in an isolation cell, left you in there for as many as thirty days, and gave you only burnt mealies to eat at every meal.

I was called and told, 'You are full of shit. You are not going to get any letters from your parents. We're going to cut your visitors.'

'Who cares?' I retorted. 'Cut my visitors, I don't need visits. Who said I need letters? I don't need to see my people, I don't need to communicate with people, I don't need your letters, I don't need anything. I'm fine here.'

'What should we do with this guy?' they started asking themselves. They didn't have the answer to that. I knew what I would stand for and what I would not, though.

I hope that bully will rot in hell or is already rotting there. When my knee got swollen at one stage, he told me: 'Tomorrow we are going to hospital. It is me and you.'

'Fuck you,' I answered, 'Go to hell.'

THE HEAD OPERATED through specialised manpower. The boys performing that function for him were the two Kleynhans brothers, who both worked as guards on the island. Although *klein* means 'small' in Afrikaans, they were anything but that. They were tall, wide, brutal Afrikaner guys with moustaches and darkish hair. Two of the most notorious guards on the island, they *looked* as if they liked abusing people. In the 1960s, they had urinated on Johnson Mlambo, a PAC member, after digging a deep hole for him and encasing him in dirt up to his neck.

One day, they came for me.

MY KNEE WAS QUITE swollen. I'm not sure how it had happened. It may have been from playing so much tennis.

'Listen, you're going to go to the hospital for your knee,' the brothers announced.

'I won't go.' I was in a lot of pain, but I refused because I didn't trust them. I didn't know what they might do to me.

'Let me talk to the doctor,' I told them.

They left and there was no doctor when they returned – just the two of them. One held me and the other started strangling me in order to place my legs in chains. He was telling me that they were obliged to put on the chains.

'If you do that, I'm going to charge you,' I told them. 'I'm going to tell my lawyer that you have been assaulting me. I'm going to charge you with assault.'

They left after that. The next day, one of them came to me and asked if he could talk to me. 'I heard you say you will charge us, but we are just doing our job,' he told me.

The fact that he had come to me was a victory for the struggle. He was giving in because he didn't want to be charged.

They were afraid.

'I don't care. I'm going to charge you. I'm not going to the hospital. I'll remain in chains until my lawyer comes here. Actually, you know what? I'm sending the word. I need my lawyer now.'

Dullah Omar was my lawyer. He became Minister of Justice after apartheid ended and served in the Cabinet from 1994 until his death ten years later. Before he became an advocate, he would come to the island and ask me if I had any grievances. He was a fighter and I liked his spirit.

The brothers knew what kind of man Dullah was. Maybe they were scared of him. They didn't like what I was telling them.

'Listen, man. Our objective is not to fight with you. We were afraid that you were going to run away,' they told me.

'But why should I run away?' I asked. 'I know why I'm here. If I run away, I'll be betraying the ideals for which I'm fighting. I'm not going to do that.'

'Are you sure?' they asked.

'What do you take me for?' I replied. 'I'm not going to run away.'

'Okay. What do you want us to do now?'

'I want to go to the hospital.'

'Do you mind if we put you in handcuffs?'

'I don't mind handcuffs, just not the leg chains.'

For us on Robben Island, my going without the chains was a big victory for the struggle. It may seem like something small, yet for us at that time it was a triumph.

Our victory was not a complete one, however. Mokgalabi was the name of another prisoner on the island. He had looted a bakery, been caught and charged with sabotage. According to the people who knew him, that was his game: he used to rob cars, rob bakeries, rob houses. He was not a member of any political organisation, just a professional thief. He started to become conscientised on Robben Island and later joined BC.

Even with his growing political awareness, Mokgalabi agreed to go to the hospital with his legs in chains. I told him that this was part of the protest we were waging on the island. 'We're not agreeing to that anymore,' I told him.

He argued with me. 'No, I agree to the chains. I don't have any issue with the chains.' I repeated that we were on a campaign, and were not going to wear chains. This time, he agreed. Maybe he hadn't wanted to take orders from someone from another party, I guessed.

But then he started telling other prisoners that I had accepted wearing chains and that he had persuaded me not to do it. Luckily, people who had witnessed our departure for the hospital stood up to him. He was a liar as well as a thief.

Adjudant, the sell-out warder who spoke isiXhosa, accompanied us to the hospital with the other guards. He was always there to listen to what you were saying and was happy to follow orders. He bought me a Coca-Cola in a false gesture of friendship. 'How many more years before I taste it again?' I asked him. 'Keep it and drink it yourself.'

When we arrived at the hospital, I found myself sitting on a bench with two older women of the sort black South Africans address as 'Mother' and treat with special respect.

You did not talk to civilians when you were on the outside. You were prohibited by law from doing this, especially if you were a political prisoner.

'Don't talk to these people,' Adjudant instructed me.

This was asking me to go against essential African norms of politeness even more so since the two women were soon asking me: 'My son, why are you wearing these clothes?'

I greeted them in isiXhosa and asked them how they were doing, hoping that this would be enough of an answer. Just then, a man who was also seated next to me tugged on my trousers and asked, 'Why are you arrested?'

I explained to him that I was a political prisoner. He wanted to know where Mandela was and I answered him. I also told an old lady who was also there: 'I'm not a criminal. I'm with Mandela in jail.'

'You must greet Mandela for us,' they all responded. Adjudant, the senior guard, was staring hard at me as I spoke. He intervened because he understood isiXhosa. After he spoke, the other guys with him moved me away from the people I was talking to even though they didn't understand what I was saying. They looked for a room to put us prisoners into so that we couldn't have contact with other people. That was too threatening to them.

A beautiful coloured woman came to take an X-ray as I was waiting for the doctor in that room. 'How are you?' she asked me.

The warders were not in the room at that moment and I said to her, 'Tell me, ma'am. There's a guy, by the name of Michael, who was a medical student here.' He was a friend of mine from Cape Town, where I'd played music before going to prison. I knew him from those days.

'Michael? I know Michael.'

'Please get him for me,' I said. 'I need to talk to him.'

THE WOMAN WENT out to looked for Michael, and he came. Sarah, the usual doctor and another friend, was not in that day. Michael started crying when he saw me.

'No, Mike. Mike, don't cry.'

'How are they treating you? We haven't read anything about you in the newspapers. Are you all right?'

No. Forget about it. Where is Sarah?'

'No, no, no. You know what I'm going to do? I'm going to make sure that we bring you back again. We'll give you a prescription that says you need to return. I'm excited, Khulu.'

'No, don't show those guys outside your excitement, or they'll never bring me back to see you.'

'Okay, let me keep my cool. I will tell our friends that I met you.'

Michael wrote a note saying that I needed to come back for another appointment. Although he was still a medical student, he became my doctor at that moment. The lady who went to fetch him made an important contribution to my life. She must be old now, and I don't remember her name. But hers was a seemingly small contribution that made a large difference. She allowed me to reconnect with my comrades. It was very brave of her because it meant taking a big risk.

THE OTHER PRISONERS wouldn't take the risk of letting you into the University of Makana right away. But when they did, they would tell you, 'How fortunate you are that out of all the people in South Africa, you have been chosen to study at this university.'

I was truly nurtured by these older people. They taught me day by day, and also night by night. They were always teaching you.

When you were walking.

When you were working.

When you were in the shower.

Even when you were about to go to sleep, they were still teaching you.

My personal tutor was an old man named Curnick Ndlovu. Short and dignified, he wore old-style black-framed glasses from the 1960s. The leaders respected Curnick a great deal. He was a trade unionist and a communist who had been arrested for sabotage activities he had committed as a member Umkhonto we Sizwe (MK). A member of the Natal Regional Command, he received a twenty-year sentence in 1963 and served all of it.

He was like a father to me.

Curnick was often alone when he was not teaching. Although he was in E Section, we still got together a lot. He taught me many things. He called economics the heartbeat of every human being and said that the section on the economy was the most important one in the newspaper.

He also taught me English. He gave me an old Royal British Dictionary with images of England as a gift. It featured the Queen's English and some Latin words.

When I arrived in prison, I spoke American slang from the movies. The older guys didn't like that. They'd say, 'What if you are called to the United Nations to represent the ANC and the country of South Africa, and you're saying, "I wanna, I'm gonna"?'

Curnick helped me with that. He also helped me to understand the history of South Africa. He said that the version we had been told – that the white man came with a Bible, that we closed our eyes to pray, and that when we opened them the country as we knew it was gone – was rubbish. 'Know the details of the country's history and you will be informed enough to understand how that fits in with the story,' he told me. 'Study how whites came here, how they operated as the coloniser.' He helped me to understand the workers' struggle and how that fits into our history, and assisted me by simplifying Marxism and Leninism for me. He spent a lot of time with me, laying down the foundations of my political understanding.

We would speak in Zulu. I didn't get what was going on when he first started teaching me by walking alongside me. I thought he was just making conversation. I understood later what was going on and appreciated all that he had done for me.

Curnick had a nickname: Nyanga Umthakathi. *Umthakathi*

means 'witch'. He accepted it when I called him Tata Nyanga, or Uncle Nyanga. I don't know how he got that name.

I have many fond memories of the time I spent with him and the moments when we laughed together. They would play the song 'Lollipop' by the Chordettes on weekends. Curnick would be twisting to it, while we younger guys would try to convince him that that dance was completely outdated in South Africa. He didn't care.

He was close to his peers, men who had been on the island since the 1960s. Old as they were, they were kept strong by playing tennis, a privilege accorded to the more senior leadership. They would compete with us young boys after we won sports privileges following our major hunger strike. Older people taught us tennis and were better than we were at the game. Mandela, Sisulu … they were all strong players. Maybe that's why they looked young when they came out of prison. We felt that we had no choice but to learn to play tennis to try to beat those older men. I didn't know about or have an interest in tennis before I got there and would never have imagined myself doing such a thing. But I started liking it out of nowhere. I got quite good at it, too.

CURNICK GOT OFF Robben Island the year before I did. I wanted clarity on something in the weeks before he left and went to him for assistance. 'Can you give me space?' he shouted at me. 'I just want to be alone.' His response shocked me because it was totally out of character.

Later he came to me and asked, 'Can I have a word with you?'

'I left my home town in 1963,' he said. 'You were not around. Let me tell you that I don't know if I have a house, or if my family is still intact. I don't know where to start. You came at the wrong time. I was busy putting my life together, so I apologise to you.'

'I don't know where to go,' he added.

I accepted Tata Nyanga's apology immediately. He died in 2002, and they named a highway after him in eThekwini. I need to go to his grave in Durban sometime.

CURNICK AND I were studying one Sunday afternoon. The warders used an intercom system with powerful speakers for the cells, and were playing Afrikaans music over it. We could not communicate because of the noise.

We pressed the button and asked, 'Can you please stop the music in our cells because we are studying?'

The warder who replied forgot to remove his finger from the button. As a result, he transmitted to all our cells the comment he had intended purely for his colleagues: 'These kaffirs, they think they are smart, you know.' Everyone heard it.

The next morning, no one was prepared to go to work when we were supposed to join our teams because of the insult. We were used to the guards using the injurious term 'kaffir' on a regular basis. That day, though, we decided to take a stand.

'We're not going to work,' was our decision.

ONE OF MY TEACHERS, Mxolisi, understood Marxism and Leninism better than anybody else in the prison. A young and vibrant member of the PAC, he read a lot and had a photographic memory. He used to tell you, 'According to Karl Marx, paragraph such and such, page such and such', and give you the quote. When he talked about *Das Kapital*, he taught you Marxist–Leninist philosophy in depth. He was the one who told me about *Grundrisse*, the book by Karl Marx. He taught me that book from A to Z just by talking to me. He spoke in a way that made me remember what he was saying. He was such a good teacher that you didn't need to read the book. By the time you opened it, he had already told you everything.

That was Mxolisi. And on the morning of that protest, he was our leader. 'We are not going anywhere until we have an apology from you guys,' he told the warders. 'You can't call us kaffirs. We demand that the guy who pressed the button and said we are kaffirs apologise. I'm demanding an apology. I'm not going to leave. Nobody is going out until that guy comes in and says sorry.'

We all agreed with him.

There was a discussion during which we could not clearly understand what either side was saying. The only thing we were sure about was that Mxolisi was speaking a strange form of English.

'Do you want to resolve the problem?' we heard the head of prison ask.

'Yes,' was Mxolisi's reply.

'Then speak English. Don't speak what you are speaking.'

Mxolisi started to laugh: 'That was classical English. I'm going to speak modern English now.'

What a character! He had been speaking Middle English, the way Chaucer spoke in *The Canterbury Tales*. I don't know how Mxolisi learned it. The funny thing is that while he was using it, all of us – including the older guys from the Makhulu Span and other older guys – pretended that we could understand what he was saying.

We know this for a fact because the old guard confessed afterwards. They had been nodding as if they understood what he was saying, when in fact they had not understood a word he had uttered.

When Mxolisi switched to modern English, the head of prison made that warder apologise for what he'd said.

We went back to work after that.

That was one form of humour on the island. We had other forms of humour, too.

Ships would pass by the island when we were at work during the day and give a tooting horn sound. Different prisoners would shout and imitate the sound. It became a norm that everyone joined, with each person doing it in their own way. The response from the prisoners would be, 'Hamba minyaka!' This meant, 'Go away, years. One day, when that horn hoots, I won't be here to hear it.'

Everybody would shout after the horn hooted.

All the guys would do it. It would happen spontaneously. If one person was standing next to you, he would move away with excitement. Then another one would move away as if they were crazy people. Soon everyone was doing it.

I guess the warders got used to it.

Together, we created a 'horn of encouragement' and a ritual for boosting morale. We gave each other energy. It didn't matter how many years they gave you, because of the courage of those guys in that moment. PAC, ANC: it was like everybody was one.

I don't think the guys in the ships who were tooting the horns ever realised what it was we were taking from their appearances. But we did.

I miss those days of shouting as if it was the normal thing to do.

We had good years and bad years on the island. But because of shared experiences like those with the tooting ships, one constant was how sad every prisoner was when he finally left.

Imagine that. A man is given his freedom and is leaving, but he's crying. He's crying because of the pain of leaving true comrades behind, because the thinking of people on the outside is often so different, and because of his uncertainty about how he will be treated there.

Exiting prisoners would leave behind everything they could: tracksuits, tennis clothes, tennis rackets and anything else they had. They would be glad that other imprisoned freedom fighters would be using the things they had left for them. These new prisoners would always find something special – sometimes even the money or other gifts your parents had sent you during your confinement. Whatever it was possible to leave behind was left behind.

That's collectivism. That was the solidarity we had. That's what used to happen. We called it *kolkhoz*, a Russian word for a collective farm in the Soviet Union.

The leaders would prepare these exiting prisoners as best they could before they left.

'Stay focused. We don't have time, time is against us,' they would say. 'When you leave this prison, you're going to be a leader on the outside. We are preparing you for this. You were privileged to be arrested, privileged to be with the people here who are teachers, who are professors, who are now going to fine-tune you.'

'When you leave here, you must know that you have graduated from the University of Makana,' they would add.

I was able to feel the difference when my graduation got closer. I was assigned to study the United Nations and learn how it operates. I needed to know about the Security Council's composition, structure and functions. That was the main task the Makhulu Span gave me.

If anybody had questions regarding the United Nations, they would call me and ask, 'Khulu, how does this department work?' I would explain it to them and they would tell me, 'Okay, you can go now.' On top of that, a prisoner named Mountain Qumbela monitored me to see if I was reading the encyclopaedia. He would read a page with me to check if I understood it.

I've never been to the United Nations in New York. I don't know if they are aware just how keenly political prisoners in South Africa studied and understood it. Maybe we could contribute to that aspect of the UN's recorded history.

I do know that, many years later, that assignment and the knowledge I gained from it on the island are still helping me. I never thought that I would be serving in the international arena, but it has helped me perform my current role as a king.

That's what being a graduate of the University of Makana means. I'm a proud graduate of that university.

The leaders would check on the exact date the sentence would end and would start to prepare the prisoner in a more detailed way as it approached. For example, they would tell him: 'When you go out, you don't talk to the media, eh? You don't talk about what goes on here.'

They would tell him which structures to affiliate to after his release. 'Before you even start to integrate into the community, go and find your leaders,' they would say. 'They will tell you who is who. If you don't do this, you'll end up working with the enemy and end up coming back here. We don't want you to come back. Look for relevant, credible people to work with. They should be the ones integrating you back into society.'

Even with these preparations, a lot of guys were so sad that they ended up shedding tears. Hard guys like Stalin, who had a prison-issue aluminium cup he loved to drink his tea and coffee from in the morning. He used to clean the cup every time he used it, and it shone so brightly it sparkled.

He said he would negotiate with the authorities to keep it. I don't know if that happened. But I do know that he was crying.

Stalin had not been involved in politics before his arrest. He had just been coming back from work when he got picked up by the police. He wanted to appeal his sentence saying that he was innocent of the politically oriented charges of which he had been accused. He was advised against appealing because doing so could lead to more years in prison.

Stalin ignored the advice and indeed did receive a longer sentence. Once arriving on the island, though, he engaged with the prisoners. They were so caring to him that he considered them his family when he left.

That's why he cried.

I cried, too, when the time came. My tears came from the sadness at leaving mixed with that feeling of excitement that comes from knowing for sure that you are heading towards freedom.

It was the same for all of us.

ON THE DAY I left prison, I was preparing to start work in the garden or at the quarry as usual. Mathumbu approached me. He was a heavy warder who smoked too much and frequently attempted to be my friend. 'You are leaving,' he told me.

'Don't joke, man. I don't have time to joke, I'm going to work.'

'No, you're not going to work. You are *leaving*.'

That was a bad thing.

You can't leave people just like that and feel good.

I was sad; everybody was sad. It was a very painful moment.

Think of the environment you find yourself in as a prisoner on Robben Island. You have a specific way of behaving and engaging psychologically, a unique and special group of people you're living with. You're thinking about all the discussions you've had with them and that you are leaving all those people behind.

That was why some ex-prisoners got themselves rearrested. They could not cope with the mentality outside. They would prefer being in prison to living outside. Many people outside were never exposed to the political realities of the day and the prisoners found it hard to relate to them.

I got the letters my mother had written to me while I was on Robben Island when I left. I'd never known she'd sent any of them because the authorities had kept every single one of them from me for the six years I'd been there. They had tried to break me, but I had beaten them.

My mother always started her letters the same way. 'Perseverance is the mother of victory,' she wrote, followed by her greeting: 'Dear Khulu.'

I read the pile of them on my way home. That was a very sad moment for me. Now that I'm older, I can better reflect on their content and my loss.

I still say that the best people I ever came across in my life are the people I met in prison. I was sentenced to ten years with four years suspended, and ended up serving the full six years. (Good behaviour did not earn you a reduced sentence when you had been convicted of political 'crimes'.)

I've never met other people so genuine, so honest, so *good*, as the people I met on Robben Island. I trusted them, I respected them, and they made me who I am. They truly initiated me. Because of this, they are the people I will always pay allegiance to.

When I met up with ex-prisoners much later in life, I used to tell them that the activists I'd met in exile had nothing on them. Basically, I regard them in the same way as I would people you might meet in heaven.

These are my people – the very best people I ever came across.

4
RETURNING TO ALEX

I came back home straight after being released from Robben Island. I had never thought in any detail what it would be like to leave prison when I was on the island. I was involved in the struggle. My concerns at the time were not about being outside. They were about how I was going to contribute to the freedom of my people.

The authorities took you to the closest prison on the mainland a few weeks before you were released. From there you'd be transferred by van to a prison in the area you came from – in my case, Johannesburg. I would be in prison in Joburg for a couple of weeks, unless I was released on appeal. I was still in jail.

I could have gone straight to Michael and Sarah if I'd been released in Cape Town. As it was, being in town until the van departed left me feeling like a stranger and totally isolated. There was no one around who knew me.

I had the same feeling of complete isolation from everyone when I left the prison in Joburg. I had been educated in a different sphere and surrounded by what had become familiar ways of doing things. I had become used to interacting in a certain way, and now I had to adjust. It was a shock to meet people I grew up with and to discover that I had nothing to say to them anymore.

It was evening when I arrived in Alex by bus from Johannesburg. My first action was to find Jingles Makgothi, the poet, at the True

Brothers butchery. We had been active politically for years together and I had always known him to write freedom poetry. He was a beautiful writer, of the calibre of Maya Angelou. He was of medium height with a sturdy build and wore dreadlocks.

I stood in the butchery for a bit. He was busy selling meat and did not recognise me at first, assuming I was a customer who needed his assistance. But he closed the butchery and started singing a struggle song as soon as he understood who I was.

We walked home and he carried my bag. My mother was hosting a church group when we got there, so we could not go in. We went to my sister Mabel's place on 4th Avenue instead. There was a problem there, too. She had a feast going, a vibe. We didn't want to just step in since there was noise and confusion. I asked a guy who was coming out of the door if he could call the lady of the house.

My sister screamed when she came out and wrapped up the event by giving away all the liquor. We walked to my mother's house and my sister just burst in. Everybody was happy to see I was home and started singing church songs. My mother shed tears as she held on to me.

A week later, the Security Branch of the police brought me a piece of paper I needed to sign. 'Do you want to sign it here or at John Vorster Square?' they asked. Naturally, I chose home. It was a banning order that required me to pledge not to participate in the activities of the ANC.

They read out the relevant clause of the Riot Act to me. It basically stated that three people (myself and two others) in one place would constitute a 'crowd' and amount to an 'unlawful gathering'. I had to ask the police for permission before going anywhere.

Then they registered our home, which entailed capturing the names and identity numbers of all family members and other people living in the house. Any outsider or visitor not on the list would be categorised as counting towards the number defined in the document.

The order stated that I was banned for ten years. If I contravened the order, I would be rearrested and imprisoned for ten years.

I signed it, but continued with the activities that had gotten me into prison in the first place. Now, though, I was 'loaded' because I had been fully conscientised on the island.

I had to find a way to sneak out of the house. One or two security guards usually stood at the front. They never found out about our back door, which was in a room we used to store older stuff. I would use that door to meet with my comrades.

I was serving with Martin Ramokgadi as part of the Transvaal High Command. I was responsible for local political education. Political education outside South Africa was John Nkadimeng's responsibility. I also served with Sheila Weinberg and Helen Joseph.

Two weeks after returning to Alex, I met with people from the South African Council of Churches in order to be briefed. They were underground members of the ANC. One of them, Delisa Mashoba, was a former prisoner. He died sometime later. I don't know how.

Delisa warned me about who was now a spy and which people it was important not to engage with. He reminded me about what I'd been told in jail: 'When you come out of jail, never work with people who have not been to prison: you'll just return to jail.'

'There's this Release Mandela Campaign,' Delisa also told me. 'You are now being deployed. The executive committee is expecting you.'

Aubrey Mokoena, Winnie Mandela and Jabu Ngwenya were among the committee members. 'You are going to create structures that will be sympathetic to ex-political prisoners, but you will also participate in the United Democratic Front,' they explained as they outlined my role.

THERE WERE NO longer any political structures in Alexandra when I was released. That felt bad as I had been used to connecting with the strong student movement we had created in the 1970s.

It was 1984, and, as could be expected, I broke that banning order to the point where they had policemen working shifts in front of my house 24 hours per day. Although they never caught me, they were aware that I was still politically active. They would refuse when I asked for permission to go to something important like the funeral of a comrade. This was particularly true if there was any chance of it turning into a political statement. If a big demonstration had been planned, they would gather known troublemakers like me ahead of it and lock us up for hours in cells in John Vorster Square before returning us home.

I would go out the back of the house before they could pick me up. The police would come in wearing balaclavas and carrying steel pipes in their hands. 'Where is Khulu?' they would say, hitting everybody in the house. This included my mother, my aunt and the many other people who stayed at my mother's house. They did not even spare the children they found there. My family would tell me what had happened after I came back to the house.

Although she was beaten regularly, my mother always supported and encouraged me despite observing a change that concerned her. 'Why do you behave like a priest?' she asked me shortly after I returned from prison.

'How do priests behave?' I retorted.

'No, man, you are rigid. You behave like somebody who, before he does anything, considers it. Before you speak, you think for a long time. The way you walk, you walk like a priest, the way you stand, the way you fold your hands. It's all like a priest. What did they do to you, those guys?'

'Nothing,'

'No, you're not the boy that left here. What did they do to you, those people?'

Older people who had been in prison would visit me at home. They came to our house because I was banned. Some came through the front, but the majority came via the back so the police did not realise that I had visitors.

One day my mother was busy ironing when two formally dressed men, Martin Ramokgadi and Kerry Seathlole, visited me. They were members of the Transvaal High Command who had come to give me an assignment in respect of the Release Mandela Campaign. They echoed what Delisa had told me: that I should not forget that I'd left people behind on the island; and that I should rally for their release.

My mother called me into the kitchen. I left these guys sitting in the lounge.

'What are you talking to these older men about?' she asked.

'No, it's okay, mama. Don't worry.'

'I don't want you to go back to prison. These people, they look like problems, like trouble.'

'No, Ma. Please, Ma. I missed you for years. I'm not doing anything.'

She didn't believe me. I explained that they were people I had been with in prison, but she guessed correctly that they belonged to a different terrain of the struggle.

'No, these guys are trouble, you can see. They dress like serious people. One is old enough to be my father. What are you doing with these people?'

I couldn't tell her: 'Yes, I'm doing wrong things again, Mama.' I was part of the High Command, which the government considered a much worse threat than before. Sometimes you hear criminals say that they've moved 'to the next level'. I was now at the highest level of criminality – as defined by the apartheid regime.

Yet amazingly, since that day, my mother would consult me every time there was a problem at home. 'There is this thing happening,' she would say to me. 'What should we do?' I would tell her what I thought, and she would thank me. She treated me like an adult. The guys from Robben Island and the High Command had helped me to graduate inside prison and at home.

THERE WAS NO DOUBT I had come from Robben Island, from people who were tried and tested freedom fighters. They were people who gave you the energy and the enthusiasm you needed to fight against colonialism. I engaged with these people – and our causes in the struggle – without experiencing any doubts. I embraced the hunger strikes, the defiance of the prison laws, and the constructive criticism that built you up.

When you came out of that environment, a tree had been planted in your mind. That tree was a tree that you wanted to water, to nurture, to grow. Whatever came to stop me was not going to succeed. That's why it was easy for me to continue living meaningfully through the enforced exile of my banning order.

OUR ASSIGNMENT WAS to remobilise the township, to return it to the level of activism reached in 1976. Alex had become quiet, and we had to start afresh, revive previous structures and create new ones.

In the period after I returned, I became acutely aware of the many types of people who opposed the struggle and worked against this intended rebirth.

You'd find among the communities a category of people who treated activists as tainted. 'Who do they think they are to challenge everything?' they would ask about us. They accepted the system and were submissive in their behaviour. The apartheid state recruited spies from this group.

There were the people who were politically ignorant or just not tuned in to what was happening. In many cases, they were men who were genuinely looking for employment. They would be promised work as a policeman and told they would not have to worry about the usual bureaucratic processes: 'Don't bring papers. We'll give you a job,' the recruiter would say.

For a guy who had little political sense, this amounted to an exciting opportunity. He would be trained for a couple of months, then deployed. He would be given the message, 'You don't work in the police station, you work in the community. You don't tell them that you're a policeman. You work underground. You get information about troublemakers and give it to us.'

You would find other people who were trained to be sent into exile to infiltrate the ANC there. They would pretend to be 'one of us'. If undetected, they would rise inside the ranks. You would take them for a genuine member after some time. The government would use the information they provided about you to monitor you.

Other informants were drawn from among tertiary students, who would be given scholarships to gather information at universities locally and internationally. Their job was to work out who the main activists – the chief 'culprits' – in that sector happened to be.

Then there were the policemen who were specially trained to infiltrate the MK ranks on Robben Island. The racist Security Branch would recruit them from among criminals in jails. 'You've got a sentence of thirty years,' the authorities would tell them. 'We will reduce your sentence and also pay you a certain amount each month if you infiltrate Robben Island.' The spies would meet their handlers by requesting a medical check-up at a hospital off the island.

'I was arrested for sabotage,' such a guy might tell you on the island when in reality he'd been arrested for robbing a bakery. There were many criminals in MK, lots of people with terrible records. A number of them were sent by the apartheid state; this group included a man from Quatro prison camp in Angola who was called Mancheck and other assassins.

You would have to look at a person's behaviour. Spies were often found among people who always made themselves available and who were keen to occupy positions. Those could be very dangerous individuals.

There were also those people genuinely living in exile who were given the mission of going back inside South Africa. MK forces had treated some of them unfairly by doing things like falsely charging them for rape and other crimes. These people joined the pool of askaris when they got back to South Africa because they wanted revenge for what had happened to them or to their comrades. Part of the struggle for some time, they had been turned aside while trying to obtain justice for themselves. They sold out because they were settling scores. Joe Mamasela, who had been part of the Mass Democratic Movement (MDM) but who came to feel that he had been betrayed by his previous comrades, was one of them.

There were those who had been part of the struggle and had turned to the enemy after being approached to become state witnesses and threatened with prison: 'If you don't, you are going to be charged – like Mandela,' they'd be told.

There were MK members who had been captured, tortured and turned. These were people who had genuinely been part of the ANC and who had been sent to work underground in South Africa. When captured by the apartheid security police, they were told stories about how their leaders were collaborating with the system; and about how the children of important ANC leaders were being sent overseas to live a cushy life. 'You are defending something that does not assist you,' they were told. Such people tended to break under such tactics, and join the growing number of askaris.

In the leadership of the United Democratic Front (UDF) and the MDM, and in some NGOs staffed by people who claimed that they held anti-apartheid beliefs, you'd also find more than a few people who were in fact traitors.

Some of the betrayals you learnt about had been imported from places of exile into South Africa. A comrade on Robben Island named Swazi, who I remember was about the same height as me, told an unnerving story about his experience following his training with MK in exile.

He had been sent back to South Africa on a mission with his training partner, 'not to fight with the gun, but to create strategic structures in Soweto'. The partner went missing just a couple of days later.

'I realised I had to move to a new address, but I got arrested before I could do it,' Swazi told me. 'While I was being interrogated at John Vorster Square, I saw my partner having tea with a Boer (Afrikaner) policeman. He was so relaxed in his company that he had his legs up on the table. As it turned out, he was a lieutenant in the Security Branch.'

'When this happens,' Swazi remembered, 'you freeze and say, "What is this?"'

His partner had walked into the room where he was being questioned: 'He was relaxed and told me, "Tell them everything. If you try to hide anything, they will just beat you up. I'm saving your life. I'm making things easier for you. They already know everything because I've told them everything. This way your life will be spared and you'll just go to jail."'

Then the partner had walked away in the company of several Boers. The guys were laughing and slapping him on the back.

SWAZI'S STORY OF betrayal by someone he thought was a comrade was far from unique. When you listened to the stories of people who spent time on Robben Island, you'd find out that most MK members there had been arrested because of a guy who'd betrayed them. Boogie Man was another example. He was a tallish, darkish guy who used to visit me a lot when he was alive. When he was sent with others from Botswana into South Africa, he was provided with the route by men he knew as senior leaders of the ANC: 'This is the route we use: from Botswana, through Bophuthatswana, to South Africa.'

Boogie Man told me, 'We each had an AK-47 and F1 grenades we called "granny's shoes" in our pockets. We were supposed to be infiltrating the air force base in Bophuthatswana. It was a suicide mission, but not one we had agreed to.'

Sensing betrayal, Boogie Man made a U-turn. 'I took another route, because I realised I would have to create my own missions,' he told me.

That's just one example of how highly infiltrated the ANC in exile was. You never knew who was who in the zoo, and deception lurked everywhere.

It lay in wait even among genuine exiles, some of whom succumbed to paranoia or to power hunger marked by cruelty. The story of Hlomuka Ngidi, a shortish, stocky guy who was part of MK's June 16 Detachment, was particularly chilling.

Hlomuka and another prisoner by the name of Nhlanhla, who recounted the story to me, were being held at Protea Police Station after being arrested. Protea was a high-security detention centre, and the two men were considered to be high-risk activists. Nhlanhla was there first and studied the routine at the station. He established that there was only one policeman in the reception area at any time. Examining the ceiling, he noted that there was a way to escape through the roof.

'If I managed to escape from Protea, I might be portrayed as a traitor,' Nhlanhla told me. 'From having been in exile, I knew how vulnerable you were if you were sent to Quatro. You could be accused of anything. I did not want to take that risk. I stayed behind because I did not want to be badly treated by my comrades in exile.'

Ngidi and others took that risk. They went through the roof and ended up in Swaziland, which was sympathetic to the ANC cause. 'How did you arrive here?' the ANC guys asked him when he arrived. Ngidi explained what had happened, and how he'd escaped.

'It's impossible,' they replied. 'You cannot run away from police custody in a high-security station like Protea.'

They shot at him and tried to arrest him, but he got away.

Ngidi exited Swaziland and travelled all the way to John Vorster Square. 'I'm one of the men who escaped from Protea. Please arrest me,' he told them. That's how he got to Robben Island: he felt safer in the hands of the enemy than with his MK comrades.

There were other, less dramatic signs that life in exile could be unusually stressful. Some of the comrades who were sent to Western countries to learn skills ended up defecting because they could not bear how terrible life was in exile. Angry and bitter, they ended up at the United Nations office, the only place they felt safe.

The ANC then took the decision not to send as many comrades to Western Europe to further their studies. They were instead sent to Eastern Europe, because the organisation knew that defection to Eastern European countries was a less attractive proposition. It was also difficult to use those countries as a launch pad for onward travel.

SHORTLY AFTER RETURNING to Alex, I was sent to Botswana to do a two-week-long crash course on ANC underground work. Martin Ramokgadi, our chair, had given me the assignment. It was a military combat course covering the techniques of working underground, including how an underground courier service works. We were also taught how to avoid getting caught by the enemy.

I travelled to Botswana via Bophuthatswana after slipping out of the back door of the family home. The police never searched the house because they never came into it in the early days of my banning order.

The instructors started the course by giving us a manual and telling us, 'Go and study this thing.' This was obviously different from being taught at the university on Robben Island.

BACK IN ALEX I also stayed at a house in Phase 2 that was owned by a principal, Mrs Manzini, who was from Swaziland and the head of Minerva High in Alex. She ran my future wife's high school and harboured me. I met her through her son, Phumuza, who liked music and liked to listen to poetry with Jingles. Little did I know that she was also an underground operative. I only understood later why we had clicked so easily.

As a result of my Botswana training I was assigned a unit in what is now North West province. At the time the area encircled the 'independent' homeland of Bophuthatswana whose president, Lucas Mangope, was widely considered an apartheid sell-out. I had to organise structures that had to fit in with the UDF's overall structure. Three of us were involved in this: me, Naude (who was also from Alex) and another guy from the area, whose name I don't remember. We went to live with him in his shack in the township of Stinkwater and started our work from there.

The guy who owned the shack was a drunkard. He did not know who we were and was mostly interested in being supplied with drink. Nevertheless, he knew the terrain well and was a good organiser. He also spoke the local languages, which were communal dialects of Setswana and Tsonga.

We needed to create structures that were specifically anti-Mangope and against the entire bantustan system in general. Putting together underground cells takes time. Naude and I followed a certain procedure in creating a new structure and finding someone to run it. You would first study a person's behavioural patterns. From there you would start engaging with them on a social, not political, basis. After a while, you would start nurturing a friendship.

You had to clear a path before you came to the conclusion that this one or that one could be trusted. As a starting point you shared with them general comments about the struggle and what it meant, and watched to see how they responded. A key moment came when they told you: 'I am sick of this situation. I want to take up arms.'

Once they had committed themselves, you would sit at the back of the venue when they attended meetings. You prepared them before meetings. If they made a mistake, you pulled them aside afterward and talked with them. Constructive criticism was key.

Sometimes I made mistakes in my choices. These were teenagers, and their parents might be warning them hard against getting involved in anything political. You had to pull away in these cases.

In Alex we worked on a number of structures, such as the Release Mandela Campaign, MK, the youth movement under COSAS, the Alexandra Action Committee (AAC) and the Alexandra Youth Congress. The work in North West was a lot more restricted. My general task was to recruit youths to fill the ranks of MK. I set up other structures at the same time as I was carrying out this recruitment work out of my love for the struggle. Naturally all of this had to be done in the most circumspect way, in line with ANC rules.

In addition to acting as the conduit for the Release Mandela Campaign in Alex, I also worked for the campaign in several other areas by going to more remote places such as Limpopo. I went everywhere I chose to go, in defiance of my banning order.

BACK IN ALEX I met with Obed Bapela, who later served as the Deputy Minister of Co-operative Governance and Traditional Affairs. Along with Jingles, we started organising ourselves. Amos Masondo, the former mayor of Johannesburg, was also involved. He facilitated a workshop on how the civic movement should be created and built, arguing that it ought to be a component of the UDF, the front that united other fronts.

There was a serious need for a civic movement. Many people were moving away from political involvement, mostly because they were afraid of being arrested. The sentences were heavy, so people had started to stay away from the struggle. We had to let them know we were still fighting.

The workshop was held near Pretoria, some 35 kilometres from Alexandra, and ran from a Thursday to a Sunday. The first unit created was a civic organisation we called the Alexandra Civic Association (ACA). We were assigned to the task together with people like Frances Baard, an ANC stalwart from the Northern Cape who was active in many areas as a member of the ANC Women's League. By the end of the weekend, we had defined everyone's responsibilities going forward.

Obed, Naude and I were responsible for creating the ACA, and we had to learn how to put together a civic organisation in a township. Obed wasn't working underground, which was a help. We also had to identify and recruit people to serve on the ACA's executive committee. Choosing the right leadership – people capable of and responsible for raising civic matters – required serious consideration. You also needed to induct them, provide them with a constitution and the correct documentation, and leave them with a workable structure.

We started implementing what is called the military art of people's war, which entailed creating street yard committees and street block committees, in that order. You chose the executive within the yard. You then moved through the houses from one corner of a block to the other, bringing people on board. Each block had to choose its own committee and executive members. All of this was supposed to happen under the ACA. Instead it took place under an alternative structure after we had issues with the Reverend Mike, whom we called Bra Mike.

We'd made a mistake in selecting Bra Mike, a reverend from the African Churches. He was bombastic and used to say things like 'The situation in South Africa is cantankerous'. We didn't know what that meant and realised he was too high-level for the task.

We'd go and confront him whenever he spoke on the podium: 'Brother Mike, we know you're knowledgeable. Please use easier words.'

'No, you're a kid, shut up. I'm in charge,' he'd reply.

Because he was so arrogant, we took the decision, 'If Bra Mike does not want to engage ordinary people, let's look for an alternative. Let's leave the civic movement with him. It will die a natural death, and we'll find another way to create another civic movement.'

Fortunately, we found Moses Mayekiso, who had been a trade unionist in the Eastern Cape and lived on 7th Avenue. A workerist and a Trotskyite, he was working with NUMSA, the National Union of Metalworkers of South Africa. He was an experienced organiser who already knew how to communicate in plain language. I also suggested Moses because we were looking for someone who was non-aligned and he was not connected to any factions. He wasn't even involved in the activities in the township at the time. He used to pass by Jingles's place of work every morning on his way to work and by Joe Manana's shop on 4th Avenue every evening. He appeared to be somebody who just woke up in the morning and went to work.

'Can I talk with you?' I asked him. I could see that he was uncomfortable, as he shivered briefly as he acquiesced.

Obed and I soon approached Moses formally about becoming the leader of the civic movement in Alexandra. Accepting meant that he would definitely end up in jail at some stage, but still he agreed.

Together we created a new structure, the AAC, under his stewardship. Naude joined Obed and me in this enterprise. I had known him for a while. He was a young chap with a vibrant personality. We would do the up and down, creating structures like the Three Musketeers.

Out of the AAC's headquarters on 7th Avenue, we were able to teach people how to create camps through which they could organise. A good deal of training on political machinery took place, and Naude and I did this. From 1st to 4th avenues was the Solomon Mahlangu camp; from 5th to 10th the Mdakane camp; from 11th to 15th the Joe Modise camp; and from 16th to 22nd the Freedom Charter camp. The people set up and ran the camps themselves.

Naude and I would dress in dirty clothes and carry sorghum beer. Disguised as hobos and drunkards, we were generally ignored and able to pass through the various boundaries of the township without eliciting the wrong kind of interest. Ironically, kids used to throw stones and tins at us, and we would duck in the street. Little did they realise that we were fighting for their freedom.

We had created youth structures even before the creation of the AAC under Moses. Ncane 'Mabida' Ntuli from Realogile High and John van der Merwe from Minerva High brought on board other Alex high schools to form the Alexandra Student League (ASL) under COSAS. We created political activity in the schools through the ASL and its leaders.

The youths of Alexandra Township also established a group called the Youth of Alexandra. Even youths who did not attend school would attend this group. They would have political discussions that I would be asked to lead. I would also invite Martin Ramokgadi and leaders from the Release Mandela Campaign to address them. The meetings were packed as the youths were thirsty for relevant information and keen to lead the fight against apartheid. We held these meetings in a church, alternating between a favourite church and other churches. There was also a youth group on 4th Avenue, which grew rapidly to needing a church on 5th Avenue, near Fifth and London roads, or what is now Vincent Tshabalala Road.

Our preferred meeting place was an indigenous church, not the Lutheran church or the Wesleyan church. It was built of corrugated iron and was owned by a reverend by the name of Baba Mbatha. That was his contribution to the struggle, which has not been recognised to this day.

We applied the military combat work (MCW) training we had received during the two-week training we had received in Botswana. My wife is a product of the training we provided during that time.

People from the civic front and from the youth participated in the political discussions. They did not seek to be elected into positions straight away: they wanted to learn and understand the struggle. They would graduate down the line. In those days, young people would say, 'I'm not ready. I'm still learning.' They had that humility.

The overall situation led to Alexandra becoming a centre for anti-apartheid organisation. We taught the M-Plan and military combat work. The M-Plan was about creating an environment that was conducive to allowing us to organise underground. We kept street yards and block committees connected so that Alex might speak with one voice. There was order in Alexandra for the first time.

A PIVOTAL MOMENT came in 1986, when a security man guarding a shop called the Jazz Supermarket shot and killed a young chap in the store. He accused the young man of having stolen a bottle of Coca-Cola and of being a 'criminal'. The victim's name was Michael Diradingwe.

The youth of Alex were ready to respond. We said: 'If we don't exploit this moment, we will not have a better opportunity in a long time. Let us implement the M-Plan. This is a good moment to mobilise the community. We need to exploit the anger and channel it into a suitable direction. We start fighting against the racist regime *now*. We start implementing the period of ungovernability in the township *now*.'

This was a most difficult moment in our fight against the regime. On the positive side the township was organised, with everyone speaking the same language. On the negative side there was a catch, which was that the community needed to be coordinated under a single umbrella so that a united leadership would be able to control it. We were in charge while leading from the back. As kids we collected money for the Release Mandela Campaign and prepared banned ANC flags for our protests. As adults we achieved total implementation of the street committees and acted as the overseers of the M-Plan.

But it was clear we had never been at the forefront. That was where Moses Mayekiso and the AAC had to come into play.

In what came to be known as Alexandra's 'Six-Day War', the anger that had been boiling for years exploded. It was anger against the police overall and against the peri-urban police specifically; and about how these forces were being mishandled as part of a campaign of systematic cruelty against black people. It was anger over many other things, too. Whatever anyone had accumulated in his or her small corner came to the surface. All that rage erupted, and the whole of Alex became involved in what followed.

Alex was a no-go area during the Six-Day War. The whole place was shut down from the outside and all normal activity stopped on the inside. The response in the initial stages following the boy's murder was not a spontaneous uprising. Along with the fact that we had politicised the youth's death and shown it as the crime it was, the MCW training and the M-Plan were the main reasons why the community heeded the call to resist.

THE SITUATION COULD have turned completely anarchic, but Alex's political organisation provided a measure of order. Yet even with this structure, an unruly crowd exploited the chaos and some opponents ended up being victims. There were police vehicles called Hippos all over the place, and some of the more disruptive elements dug holes in the middle of roads to trap the vehicles, covering them with corrugated iron topped with sand to disguise them. Policemen would fall from the trapped Hippos. The people would disarm and even kill those fallen men. There were also young boys who used slings and iron balls to hit the police. They would buy bolts and nuts at a hardware shop run by Chinese people to hit the Hippos as they were passing by.

The streets in Alex did not have electricity and were never tarred in those days. Their surface was gravel, there were few street signs, and there was a feeling of sameness everywhere. Something important changed at the time of the six-day battle. Blood was on the gravel and the smell of ammunition was everywhere. It was a war zone, like Beirut in the '70s and '80s.

THE SHOOTING AND killing went on for the full six days and involved both youths and parents on one side and the security forces on the other. The police killed many people. There was a mass funeral in Alex for the victims, at which more than twenty people were buried. That number was the official total of people killed. It could have been higher – some people estimated that nearly forty people had died in the township.

The government didn't like us making the system ungovernable because they knew that our larger objective was to get rid of apartheid. They were looking for the leaders and got to some of us. Moses Mayekiso, Obed Bapela and others were arrested in June 1986 and tried – though unsuccessfully – for treason, subversion and sedition.

MY MAIN HOPE AFTER these terrible events was for visibility for the Alex victims' mass funeral. We went to the headquarters of the Release Mandela Campaign in central Johannesburg to ask for help: 'We need your participation. We need a flag. We have structures in place, but people need more support than they can provide.'

There was a meeting at the headquarters to talk about the logistics of the funeral and how Winnie Mandela and other leaders would get there. I was on the exec of the Release Mandela Campaign at the time. I went disguised as a hobo in the back of a van. Winnie was there when we arrived. She, Aubrey Mokoena and I were responsible for all of Alex when it came to the campaign.

We needed to send flowers to pay homage to those who had been killed. There was a discussion about a donated wreath which was to consist of fresh flowers in the ANC colours. It could not be brought in during the meeting for me to take home, as this posed too much of a risk to the people at the meeting. We thus needed to smuggle those flowers into Alex shortly before the funeral.

Winnie Mandela proposed that the best option was to let the wreath sleep at my family home since it was the only house to be trusted in Alex. Police no longer stood guard because I'd been hiding at different addresses and was never there.

I had to agree that there was no alternative house to take them to. They were going to arrive in a 1400 Datsun van the evening before the funeral. I had to split myself in two in terms of the funeral arrangements, and to enter my mother's and my sister's place carrying a wreath in the ANC colours.

If those flowers were found in my room, it would mean ten years' imprisonment. We had to find a way to put them in my sister's room instead. As the last step in this elaborate plan, Winnie and Ismail Ayob would pick up the wreath from my house and go straight to the stadium with it.

It was suicide.

WINNIE ARRIVED AT our house in the morning. My mother stopped doing the washing and made tea before they talked outside in the yard. There was a feeling of chaos everywhere, but the two of them just chatted away as if nothing at all was happening.

'What is this now?' I thought to myself, feeling very much on edge. Winnie was Winnie. She inevitably attracted the police and the media. I have never seen a woman like that one.

I was in the car by then and we went to the stadium in our role as organisers of the mass funeral. No one stopped us.

I reminded her about the mass funeral and the wreath years later. Ahmed Kathrada, Winnie and I were attending the ceremony held to formally receive the repatriated remains of JB Marks and Moses Kotane, two activist icons who had been buried in Moscow and were reburied on South African soil in 2015. 'It was just part of the struggle,' she laughed.

I REMEMBER MANY other things clearly from my life in Alex during my house arrest. At the time before the Six-Day War when the structures we had set up were still intact and functioning, ANC President OR Tambo issued a clarion call for a consumer boycott.

What do we do? we asked ourselves. Who was going to act as chair? It was a risky game.

When Obed said, 'My hands are full,' I decided that I would take the risk, act as chair and make it happen. This involved talking to black and Indian consumer associations to ask them to lower their prices so that people would buy at their shops rather than from the large, mostly white-owned supermarket chains. I met with the Alex Chamber of Commerce and the Indian Trade Association, and they agreed to come on board. The boycott was effective and for a time we crippled an important part of the racist regime's economy.

THERE WERE ARRESTS, detentions, and then a first state of emergency in July 1985. It initially covered some 36 magisterial districts in the industrial heartland of South Africa (Gauteng) and the townships that serviced it, and in the Eastern Cape. The town of Cradock in that province was another place that had come to know the state's loathing towards activists and was fighting back.

Alex was a burning township, but we just kept on pushing. We did not know then that the enemy would give up in 1990.

The boycott got out of order. Some youths stopped parents carrying supplies bought from Pick n Pay, one of the largest supermarket chains. They would make them drink whole bottles of fish oil and swallow Omo washing soap on the spot, to punish them for buying from white store owners and to persuade them never to do that again.

We talked to the youth about this behaviour through the

courts we had established. By that time, the AAC had taken over the community. We had created our own system of governance in Alex. For instance, we had put together our own police contingent, which consisted of comrades and dedicated marshals whom we sent to spots where there were incidents. Alex's main 'police station' was now on 7th Avenue.

People would not want to go to the apartheid courts when they had grievances. To keep order in the community we established what we called a 'People's Court', also operating from 7th Avenue. Such courts remained in place for quite a long time, until about 1991 or 1992. They used to deal mostly with minor issues – problems in a yard, fighting between families, or children not behaving well. A mother might say, 'You know, my child drinks liquor. My child does not do as I say.' The People's Court would discipline the child.

There was also a unit established by the People's Court through which a number of older youths were assigned to check on all those youths who were drinking liquor at a tender age. Every night, and even more on weekends, they would check every place where alcohol was sold. If young kids were there, the older ones would usually deal with them by beating them.

We held workshops for the comrades we had chosen. They were taught how to run the courts at these sessions and came to understand how the judiciary works. These people became our magistrates and prosecutors. Some NGOs volunteered to train our presiding officers. Sometimes our judges who were not trained had been drawn from the ranks of credible elderly people.

Cases ran every day, until late. The AAC educated presiding officers about the aim of the court. This training was critical. 'Hey, comrade, you're going to be doing the following,' these officers would be told. 'When there is a hearing, you must make sure that you are in charge. Bring this one and that one to assist you, and follow this procedure.' That's how we established our court.

We created a charge office, too, for people to come to. If someone laid a complaint against you, people would be sent to look for you throughout Alex. The court would listen to the case and judge it based on its merits.

Naude and I never sat in those courts as we were operating underground. At a certain point, however, we got worried because we heard that there were complaints in Alex. Many people were saying that people were being beaten purely on the basis of being accused.

The People's Court was becoming a kangaroo court, and this was giving the AAC a bad name.

As the architects of the People's Court, we felt that we had allowed this nonsense by not paying proper attention to what was happening. It was up to us to end it.

The guys who were running the court did not know us because we were 'on the UG', meaning that we were underground. At times there was looseness, there was ungovernability, and there were things that were just plain wrong.

When this happened, you had to get back to the marshals. Sometimes, if the situation called for it, you would break the invisibility code to restore order, after which you would go back underground. They did not know who the architects of the system were and believed *they* were in charge. At those points, we had to infiltrate them and bring back order. When things were settled, we would leave people with properly defined responsibilities in terms of operating the court or other structures, and would return to our underground lives.

On the occasions when we were forced to intervene, Naude and I would go and listen throughout the proceedings. We would explain to the youth, 'Your purpose here is to re-educate these people so that they can again be part of society. Your purpose is not to punish by hitting them with sjamboks.'

There was, for example, a case involving an old isiXhosa-speaking lady whose complaint was that her daughter did not respect her. The mother had brought a case against the daughter and young boys had beaten the daughter with a sjambok. We explained carefully: 'Don't do this. The main objective of this place is to rehabilitate people, not to beat them. If you're going to be beating people, they will not have confidence in you and you'll not be able to assist them in changing their lives.'

When things went as they should, people who had been accused of wrongdoing would be brought to the court unhurt by youths intent on keeping order in the township. Elderly people whom the youths respected would serve on those cases. Occasionally, we would give input on who should preside over a case. If the accused was an elderly person, or if the case was between a parent and a child and involved a question of lack of respect, only an older person would be allowed to deal with it. The decision had to be a sober one for the court to have credibility.

But there was no restraint when it came to traitors. The People's Court did not deal with them. They had a petrol-soaked tyre placed around their neck and set alight with a match. It was a tool used at the time to deal with enemy agents.

We had started reading General Giap's book, *The Military Art of People's War*. From our reading, we began to view every rudimentary weapon that was at our disposal as a legitimate way of liberating ourselves. Although we felt that we had to use the available weapons, we never actually pronounced on necklacing.

Although our policy on this was vague, the necklacing of a girl in Alex named Teresa was anything but nebulous. Wherever there were young girls or boys, Teresa would be found mingling with them. I never encountered her, but people said that she would approach each child with, 'Hi, comrade, what is your name?'

Straightaway that was suspicious, as we never called each other by name. Having learnt the law of secrecy during MCW, we simply said 'Comrade' or 'Com'.

That was all. We didn't want to know anyone's name or address. Where someone lived was none of our business. Teresa wanted the details and would write them down.

People started saying, 'No, man.' When a group of them decided to approach her about her behaviour, she ran away. Her flight from Alex was taken as proof that she was part of the Special Branch and that she had pointed activists out to the government. One day she made the mistake of returning to the community. She was captured and burned alive.

The same thing almost happened to Sam Ndaba. Sam had married an aunt of Connie Bapela, Obed Bapela's wife. Naude trusted him because they had grown up together. He stayed on 14th Avenue and was also a participant in the Youth Congress. Little did we realise that he was a policeman feeding information to the enemy. He infiltrated the ANC underground, taking ordinary ANC members and guerrillas underground with him.

Sam was part of our group while we were planning a stayaway in Alex in 1985. We had been in Botswana and had come back to Alex for that purpose. Sam met with Obed and we started to plan. We had no idea we were dealing with a traitor.

Sam sold out one of my colleagues, Vincent Tshabalala, who had gone to Angola, trained there and come back. We all met at the Indian-owned shops. Sam was hosting Vincent and two other comrades at the time. He had our trust. In fact, the ANC believed him to be an MK soldier responsible for other MK soldiers coming into South Africa on missions.

No one suspected that Sam was a policeman, but he ended up being a Special Branch security officer. When he was outed, he was seized and set alight. He didn't die because Special Branch colleagues who were in the area rescued him. The only part of him that burned was one of his ears. He was totally open about being a policeman after that.

One of the aspects of the secrecy we practised related to the use of code. We would pass on messages through Martin Ramokgadi and Muzi Kubheka, making in-person meetings unnecessary. We would take all the matches out of a matchbox, put the message in the box and refill the box. You would keep the master copy in a secret place at home. Everyone involved knew how to decipher the message because we shared the code.

It was a simple enough code to master:

The number 2, for instance, might stand for the letter B.

The number 100 might stand for A.

The number 20 might stand for F.

The number 200 might stand for E.

And 49 might stand for L.

We would write the following on a piece of paper: 2 100 = 20; 200/49/200, which spelled the word 'BAFELE'. We would then place this in the matchbox we had prepared for the task.

The message might be meant to alert the recipient that a person had died or that they must leave the country at once. We had a limited range of predetermined messages, but the system was an efficient one.

You would drop the box when the intended recipient or courier was only some ten feet from you. The delivery worked as follows:

I drop the message on the ground.

I don't even look at you.

I keep walking and I'm gone.

You pick up the message.

Naude and I had this kind of underground meeting most of the time, both as a useful shortcut and because we never walked if we could avoid it. The Special Branch guys would drive around with their spies in their silver Toyota HiAces with tinted windows. It was not easy.

Nevertheless, we remained 100 per cent committed. Naude and I never slept for long and never had time for girlfriends while we were fighting for our freedom in Alex. When I'd see beautiful girls at night and want to talk with them, the first thing I would think was, 'What if this person ends up compromising me?'

I saw black women and thought, 'They are my sisters.' Getting involved with them would not have been right. It was too close. It never came into my mind to have a woman at my side, or even to have sex. The main issue was to liberate South Africa.

That was it.

Before going to prison, I'd had a girlfriend in Cape Town named Anne Dolores, who loved me very much. She was white and spoke up for me at important moments.

One night, when I was tired after playing a gig, I took her to the station so that she could catch the train and go home. As we were waiting for the train, I was overwhelmed by the desire to sleep. She said, 'Then sleep here, Khulu.' While we were waiting, I rested my head on her lap.

Two railway policemen appeared and didn't like what they saw. '*Fuck* you,' they told us. We were on railway territory and thus were subject to their jurisdiction.

Anne would have none of it. 'This is my husband,' she said. 'I'm from England. I'm going where I want to go. Fuck *you*.'

She turned to me and said, 'Khulu, you must stay here and leave only when the train comes.'

When the train pulled into the station, she kissed me in front of those guys. I walked to the exit and left. Although the guys were very unhappy and made negative comments, they did nothing more.

I owe Anne a lot, but it was a matter of 'Revolution first'. As I write about this, I am reminded of reading about Ernesto 'Che' Guevara's life. When Che had to make a choice between the revolution and his wife, he chose the former.

We did the same.

OBED, JINGLES MAKGOTHI and I used to recruit a lot of young men on 17th, 18th and 19th avenues in Alex. Jingles was a poet and a member of the Khawuleza Cultural Ensemble. We loved each other.

We would recruit people by engaging with them. Jingles and I used to work at a butcher shop along with other guys from MK, where I pretended to be a professional meat cutter.

We would check each candidate's family first. We needed to be sure that it was not the kind of family that could send us to jail.

Once we determined that they were ready, that was it. We took a lot of them across the border to join MK.

The government naturally regarded us as terrorists and had a number of people out to get us. Some of them were Inkatha Freedom Party (IFP) members who lived at the Madala Hostel and stored ammunition there. The IFP was in cahoots with the racist regime. It also bought off some members of the Azanian People's Organisation (AZAPO), who started killing people for them.

Jingles was the easiest of targets. He was always at the butcher's, and they shot him and killed him as he was closing the shop door. They killed him right outside the entrance to the Madala Hostel in Alex.

Naude and I had warned Jingles about this that morning. He wanted to attend the funeral of Victor, a friend and an AZAPO member. 'You can't go because they will eat you alive,' we told him. We said this because of the tension that existed, right then, between the United Democratic Front (UDF) and AZAPO, which was aligned with Black Consciousness.

'I'm going for a jog,' I said as I left him. 'I'll find you when I get back.'

I never saw him again.

After Jingles was killed there was a riot on 12th and 13th avenues, where the houses of Black Consciousness (BC) people were situated. I believe that the security forces, in tandem with the IFP, were the ones who killed him. Other people claimed that AZAPO did it. At some stage, it was decided that BC houses as a whole had to be attacked because it was BC that had killed Jingles. While Black Consciousness had been strong in the 1970s, the UDF had taken over in terms of prominence by the 1980s. They had done this because Jingles was a UDF guy, some people argued, and revenge had to be exacted.

It was extremely hard to make one's way through political accusations in the 1980s. Things were often murky. The Special Branch had become greatly invested in fomenting strife between the different liberation movements. Some of its members started wearing UDF t-shirts to pretend that they belonged to the organisation and would then attack AZAPO activists while wearing these t-shirts, sowing fear and uncertainty.

Despite this confusion, it was felt that we had to avenge Jingles and attack AZAPO houses. We threw bombs at them. It was a bad thing to do, yet at that moment we convinced ourselves that we had no other option. I was told that some of the guys we had trained went there later in the day, confronted some of the AZAPO men and shot at them. I was also told that one AZAPO member was shot at daybreak. They put a gun in his mouth and blew him away.

Around September 1986, I got instructions to go to Botswana. When I was there, I was told I had to attend a crash course in the

Soviet Union. Naude had been trained there earlier in political machinery, which included propaganda methods. His specialty was creating structures and units, or what we called 'cells'. He had also learned about publishing and distributing propaganda materials, including by means of pamphlet bombs.

Leaflet and pamphlet bombs were best let off at busy spots where a lot of people were gathered, like bus stops at peak hour. They would make a big bang and scatter the leaflets all over. People would start picking them up to read then or later.

Naude and I had released these harmless pamphlet bombs regularly, at over a dozen different bus ranks.

When the ANC was unbanned, Naude became head of Political Education for the ANC in Gauteng. He recruited Zweli Sizani and me to serve on that body.

NAUDE AND I GREW bored after I returned from the Soviet Union to Botswana after my crash course. He was restless and had not even wanted to attend a new short course in Russia. The idea was that we would stay in Botswana and work for the struggle from that country. But we decided to go back to Alex and to do this without telling anyone.

In the meantime, the people of Alex had decided to come together and take part in what came to be called the March of Alexandra. They were going to march from Alexandra Stadium to the police station in Wynberg.

In those days, organisers would come and knock on your door: 'Every man, out. Every woman, out.' They would force out everybody capable of walking, even children, to participate. The older youths would look after the younger ones. Everybody had to be part of the war.

So, on that day in late 1986, almost every single person in Alexandra joined the march. The security forces were also out in force.

When Naude and I arrived in Alex between 5 pm and 6 pm, we started shooting randomly at the security forces with Makarov pistols to force them to run away. We'd connected with our secret suppliers after arriving without any firearms in Johannesburg.

This new confrontation was the first time that the ANC Command knew that we had moved back to Alex. They initially had no idea who was responsible for organising it.

ANC directives always told us to send a code to Botswana to claim responsibility for any act that we were directly involved in. When we claimed responsibility, Chris Hani told us that we had done wrong. 'You need to come to Lusaka,' he ordered.

We couldn't understand where we'd gone wrong. We were under great pressure in the world, and every force was out looking for us: the police, the devil and God. Naude was sure he did not want to be in Zambia. 'We must fight. The revolution is here,' he kept saying.

We decided to stay, as we were in a mess no matter what.

AROUND THE SAME time, Naude started to contemplate recruiting someone named Tekere from Alex. He was one of the members of the Youth Congress, an affiliate of the UDF.

'I must go and meet Tekere,' he told me.

'Why do you have to meet Tekere?'

'I know Tekere. We grew up together in the Congress.'

I had never liked the guy. He always wanted to be involved in every activity going. He was too available. He also used to dress up in green khakis as if he were in the military. He would say things to us sometimes that made me ask, 'How does he know that?'

One day he came and confronted me during a night vigil at an African Methodist Episcopal church.

'I know you are a MK soldier,' he said.

'What is MK?' I asked. 'What do you know about MK?'

'Please hook me in.'

'Hook you into what?'

I had understood that this guy was not a safe bet. Naude was arrested on a street corner in Alex in front of a house where he'd had his meeting with Tekere. I had told him not to go to the meeting that afternoon. He had not listened to me.

I saw it happen, as I was there with a comrade from Pretoria. The two of us had talked about Naude going to that house and meeting with Tekere, and had agreed to hang around on the street in case things went south.

We stood briefly on the corner before slipping into someone's yard to hide. From there we had to watch Naude get taken away in handcuffs. He was being pulled by his pants towards an unmarked car. There was nothing we could do.

It was also painful to realise that we, too, were no longer safe. We knew that when a comrade was arrested, the chances were high that you would go to jail as well. It was easier that way because you didn't have to spend your energies wondering about getting caught or not. As long as the sentence was not a lengthy one and you did not get arrested again, you could carry on operating after you came out of jail. The struggle had to continue.

WHEN A COMRADE was arrested, he had to try to hold out for the next 24 hours. He might break after that point, but he had given you the opportunity to get away.

Naude held out. We had left for Botswana right away, using our own route through Bophuthatswana. We fetched some young people on the way who were going into exile. 'Guys, let's do the trip now,' we told them. When they agreed, we started looking for a kombi.

I SAW NAUDE AGAIN years later in Angola, when I was deployed to Amandla because I was no longer politically relevant. A driver in a truck had come to pick something up, and Naude was there by chance. He was living in Viana camp and working on the docks in Luanda, where he would pick up ammunition for MK.

I caught sight of him at the back of the truck, waiting to be dropped off at the docks. We embraced and laughed. I asked him what had happened after his arrest.

'I knew I had to hold on for 24 hours, but these guys never had a case,' he told me. 'They held me for about seven months without charging me, so I was let out.'

They had arrested him with no incriminating evidence on him. They had held him because they'd heard that he had attended a crash course in Botswana, not because of MK activities. 'I went for the course, but I'm no longer interested in that,' he told them. He was subjected to continual interrogation even though that was all they'd been looking for.

'Now I'm here to do the military training,' he told me with a smile.

I WASN'T SMILING THE evening that Jingles was killed. I had decided to go for a run, and it turned out that my route took me right next to the spot where I was about to be shot. Maybe my plan had been to run towards Louis Botha Avenue. I don't recall exactly. I do remember that I had come down from Alex, past a row of shops, and turned right onto Wynberg Road in the direction of Bramley.

Near Eden College, I went down into an area that was covered in darkness. I was used to it, as I often ran there. A white woman who was driving through must have seen me as a vague shape in the darkness: she shone her brights to make sure there was no obstacle in her path. In their light I saw a powder-blue Sierra. Close to it were two people with balaclavas wearing black clothes and carrying short-range guns. They were partly hidden behind a tree, waiting for me to come up to their level. In the same flash of light, I recognised a white Afrikaner policeman who had harassed us. He was still visible despite having squeezed in between two trees on the side of the road.

I would have died that day without those brights. Those guys must have been following me to make it look as if I'd been killed by criminals. It was a good opportunity for them because there would have been a lot of speculation about what exactly had taken place if I'd died in Bramley.

I made a U-turn and ran as hard as I could. Luckily, I was fast in those days. I jumped a brick wall, climbed to the second floor of an apartment complex, and knocked on a door. I felt close to crazed. A white man who was wearing shorts opened the door. I told him that I was a political activist and that people wearing black clothes were waiting for me with guns to kill me. He went to talk with another white guy, and they took a car down the road to confirm what I'd been saying.

When they returned, he said: 'It's true. Where do you live?' I told him 4th Avenue in Alex, and they asked where the safest place would be for them to drop me off. I told them Alex Clinic on Arkwright Avenue, which was safer for white people because it was on the outskirts of the community. They dropped me off, turned and drove back to where they lived. I only reflected after the incident that he could have been a policeman or might have asked himself afterwards why he chose to help me.

I also pictured what easily could have happened to me without their help. 'This is where I could have been, on the ground, with my blood ebbing away next to those trees where they were hiding,' I thought.

Those three white people saved my life that night.

Relief flooded over me at my narrow escape. But when I came back and told my sister the story, she said, 'Don't go to the butcher. Jingles was shot just now.'

The butcher's store where he'd worked was the first place I'd gone to when I'd returned to Alex after six years on Robben Island. He was the first person I'd gone to see. That's how close I was to him.

I was denied permission to bury him. The police buried him instead. Devastating.

Soon after these events I left for Angola to fight against the UNITA[3] rebels. Jingles's murder and the attempt on my own life had occurred in the month before I went into exile. I was training to make sure that I was fit and had built my stamina. I did not know what six months of military training were going to require of me, and needed to prepare myself properly.

I now wanted to make a full-time commitment. I felt that I had played my part in recruiting the youth into the struggle and wanted to join MK. What I had given thus far was not enough: I wanted to make a greater contribution to the cause of freedom.

That meant facing the high probability of losing my life. I wanted

---

3   National Union for the Total Independence of Angola

to see action, and that meant confronting the enemy and fighting. I was ready.

I had taken my decision after witnessing an incident involving two Afrikaner youths sitting on top of a Hippo on the corner of Ruth Street and 5th Avenue. They were having a discussion about shooting a child in the head. A real child, who was playing soccer with other children in the street.

One of them was saying, casually, as they were sitting there: 'I could shoot that one in the head.'

Seconds later, he shot the boy as if doing so meant nothing to him. Then they drove away, leaving the child on the ground to die.

I had no other choice than to seek revenge for that boy.

5
ANGOLA

When I left for Angola, I did not go alone. Four of my comrades who were recruited by the Transvaal High Command – Meshack Nhlapo, Cyril Pitso Jomo, 'Bricks' Makofane and 'Deddy' – went together with me. We travelled north to Rustenburg then on to Botswana, entering that country through the fence near the Phitshane Molopo border post.

We decided to declare our presence in the country at the police station in the town of Lobatse. They made us stay in the Lobatse prison, which they said was a safe place to sleep over the weekend. They drove us on the following Monday to the local commissioner of police.

He yelled at us at first: 'You are informers. You are traitors.' He pulled us aside and asked who the leader was. My comrades all pointed at me.

The commissioner explained that he had to make sure we had not been sent as spies by the racist Afrikaner government. I told him that I had done my research and that we were tried and tested freedom fighters. He accepted that, although I don't know what intelligence he based that on, and asked us to write detailed biographies. They had to have a record of us as refugees. We had to tell them information like where we came from, who we were and what we were doing in Botswana. We were allowed to move on after that. We stayed in

Gaborone before being given tickets to travel to Francistown many miles away. Francistown was the gateway to the Dukwi refugee camp, which housed members of the South West Africa People's Organisation (SWAPO), the ANC and BC.

Once in Francistown, we again reported to the Botswana police. They were soon trying to connect with the United Nations to ask them to pick us up and take us to the camp. The United Nations Refugee Commission ran a truck service that drove between Dukwi camp and Francistown for refugees who needed to buy food and other basic supplies with the money they received as an allowance from the United Nations.

'Who do you want to meet at the camp?' the Francistown police asked us as we waited. When we said the ANC, they seemed to feel that meeting with the ANC would prove to be very difficult. One policeman told us about Ntate Nthithe, an old man who had left South Africa in the 1960s. 'He might be of assistance to you,' he said, giving us directions as to where we might find him.

Ntate Nthithe, we discovered, had come from Alex to join the ANC in the 1960s. He told us that he had been a member of the Youth League with Mandela in the 1940s.

He listened to us and asked, 'Are you sure that you want to join the ANC in Angola?'

'Yes, people are dying at home,' we replied without hesitation.

'I hear you,' he said, looking directly at us. 'If I were you, I would take a scholarship when I arrive at the refugee camp and become a non-aligned person.'

That was the first time I learned that there were non-aligned people living outside South Africa who were going abroad to study.

'I would take a UN passport and forget about this,' he concluded.

'Why?' we wanted to know.

'These people are not right,' he responded. 'You will regret it. They are not good-hearted people.'

That was the only time we spoke with Ntate Nthithe. I heard later that he had ended his days in Francistown.

OUR ENERGY AND revolutionary spirit made us not want to listen to him. We wanted to fight for South Africa and believed that only the ANC could provide that opportunity. This was the main reason we went back to the police station in Francistown and tried to connect with the Dukwi refugee camp for several days. The people at the camp informed the Botswana police that they didn't know anything about us, and therefore would not be able to let us in. When we tried to force ourselves onto a truck that was going there, the driver told us we were not allowed on it because we were not on his list of passengers. Refugees from Zimbabwe and Namibia were on the truck.

We went back to the police station and told them that we would wait some more. They had allowed us to have proper shelter and sleep on the floor of a room that was both library and meeting room. But the arrival of a group of young white female tourists at the station led the police to say that we would have to sleep outside in tents. The women needed proper accommodation to avoid being subjected to crimes such as rape.

It was clear that we would have to make way for them. When we went outside, however, we found that the tents the police had mentioned did not exist. 'Let's try again to get onto the transport to the camp,' we decided the next morning. This time, there were three South African guys from the Eastern Cape on the UN truck. They spoke up for us and convinced the driver to take us to Dukwi.

Many people from the Francistown community shouted at us in Tswana as the truck was passing them: 'People who cross the fence!' They were telling us that we had run away from our country and had crossed the border fence illegally. Their shouts echoed from each and every corner.

AN ANC REPRESENTATIVE interviewed us once we reached Dukwi camp, a two-hour drive from Francistown. We also had to provide our biographies anew. The ANC would cross-check what you wrote in your biography with what you said in your interviews to make sure that you were legitimate. Members of Imbokodo, the ANC's security cluster, had been trained in these tactics by the East Germans, the Soviets and the Cubans. The aim was to identify possible traitors to the cause. To our youthful minds, it was irritating to have to supply the same information over and over. Only later did we realise how useful it was to root out people who had been sent by the enemy. I understood the need better when I did my training in military intelligence in the Soviet Union and, after that, when I was the head of protocol for the Amandla Cultural Ensemble.

We slept in tents that night and were then transferred to a house, where our main worry was who was going to be cooking and washing the dishes. They asked us if we wanted to go to school or to the army. Bricks said that he wanted to go to school and we told him that he was betraying the people of South Africa.

'Why are you turning now?' we asked him.

'What if I die?'

We told him he was a coward. He eventually changed his mind and trained with us.

IMBOKODO CLEARED US and some weeks later we were advised we were going to Angola for military training. Before long they had organised passports for us and told us that we would be travelling by train from Botswana to Zimbabwe.

Mike, a guy who was missing his right hand, picked us up from the station in Zimbabwe and drove us straight to the ANC office in Harare. In the afternoon we were taken to the Zimbabwe–Zambia border in a kombi driven by Jabu Moleketi, who became a deputy minister of finance under Thabo Mbeki in 2004. We did not sleep that night. We ate and rested a little before driving straight to the Chirundu border post.

The Zambian side of the border was closed when we arrived. Our ANC colleagues appeared to be unaware of this and drove off in their kombi once they saw us approaching the authorities on the Zimbabwean side.

Even if the Zambian border post had been open, we would have encountered a second barrier to our entering the country: border control there hadn't received the communication they required from the ANC people on the Zambian side.

It was a trying night. We didn't have any food supplies and later it rained, drenching us all in the nearby wood. We had no matches, either. A guy from a nearby village who was passing by on a bicycle gave us a few. It still took until midnight for the wood to dry.

Our fortunes improved after that. On a walk to take a look at the nearby Zambezi River, we found dead sardines on a bank. For some reason the fish had leapt out of the river. We picked them up, fried them on the fire, and settled down in a dirty room to sleep.

In the morning, ANC members sent from Lusaka came to fetch us in a kombi. We walked to the Zambian side. The authorities there stamped our powder-blue passports and drove us from the Zambian border to Lusaka, the capital. We passed through a prominent district in the city called Makeni on the way. We then received new names. My *nom de guerre* was Sandisile, which in English means 'elongated' or something that is to be continued or extended.

WE ARRIVED IN LUANDA, Angola, in the early hours of the morning. Pure joy surged through us at having made it to a Marxist country and at seeing murals featuring iconic figures like Lenin, Karl Marx, Dos Santos, Agostinho Neto, Fidel Castro, Che Guevara and various people holding an AK-47. 'We are real revolutionaries now,' we told ourselves.

The country was beautiful, too. Angola has a tropical climate that is always hot and humid. Its fertile soil contains so many bushes and so many trees close to each other that you'd find yourself walking into walls of green vegetation. You would also find diamonds just lying on the ground. At the time we didn't understand that they were precious stones. They just seemed ordinary to us. One of our comrades used some of them to decorate his room, but he didn't bother to take any back to South Africa.

Despite Angola's physical beauty and my belief that I was fighting for my country and my people, I quickly learned that life in MK was completely different from life on Robben Island. I had been educated politically by humble people who had made me love the ANC. Those Robben Island people were incredible role models for me.

After leaving that inclusive, caring and collaborative environment with people who never held grudges, I always felt inspired – through the memories and lessons I carried with me – to continue with the struggle to free my people. I had expected to experience the same kind of understanding between comrades when I had joined the ANC underground on being released from Robben Island, and that expectation had by and large been fulfilled.

Angola was completely different. Although you had to prove yourself during that six-month waiting period on Robben Island, the leadership didn't make you feel isolated, or as if they believed you were a suspect. You were part of the scene even if you were not yet part of the 'ring of comrades'. In Angola, on the other hand, you rapidly realised that you were being viewed with suspicion. As time went on, you understood that this disturbing atmosphere was a constant reality.

On the island you could engage, argue – and even fight. You had the freedom to raise things you thought were wrong. In Angola the organisation was a purely military one where you just took orders. That was the extent of your contribution.

'Don't question. You question, you go to jail,' was the unwritten rule. They would lock you up in a metal container, as they did with me when I was accused of rape.

Dislike and jealousy could easily lead you into trouble. Total isolation would begin to envelop you the minute you were under suspicion, even if it was based entirely on unsubstantiated accusations. People would move away from you whenever you sat down anywhere. The end result was an ugly kind of silence. Even though you saw atrocities happening in your presence, you were denied the right to stop them because of what would happen to you.

The leaders didn't want any questions. 'You comply now, then you can complain later,' they would declare. We soon realised that it was no use, as 'later' never came. Joseph Nxumalo, famously known as 'General', learned the truth of that. MK members shot him in an assassination attempt because he asked why our soldiers were in the camps rather than out fighting. His saga began when he saw that many people who were sent to the Soviet Union for training did nothing once they got back to Angola. He raised the issue of why

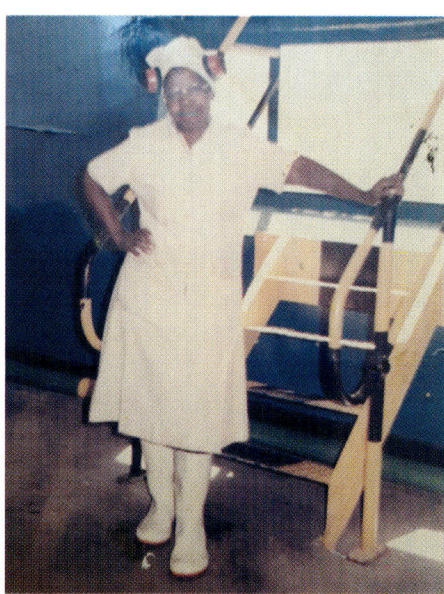

Top Left Gaur Radebe, my grandfather, was one of Nelson Mandela's mentors.

Top Right My mother told me I looked like a priest after I returned from Robben Island.

Bottom Left My mother's deep spirituality is shown by her regular attendance at the indigenous church of Zion.

Bottom Right My mother, Mariam Radebe, was a supervisor at Farm Fare, a company that packaged chicken.

Top Left I'm with a friend at a reception for Amandla in Tokyo, Japan.

Top Right I was performing with bass player Sipho Gumede in a band formed by Jonas Gwangwa at a concert called 'Heal Yourself'.

Left These are the percussionists from the Amandla Cultural Ensemble, who toured using music to contribute to fight for freedom.

Bottom Left Glen Mariko, Johnny Mekoe, Enoch Mthalane and I were in a musical group organised by Amandla Cultural Ensemble leader Jonas Gwangwa.

Bottom Right I am in Singapore with Sis Esther, one of the singers in the Amandla Cultural Ensemble.

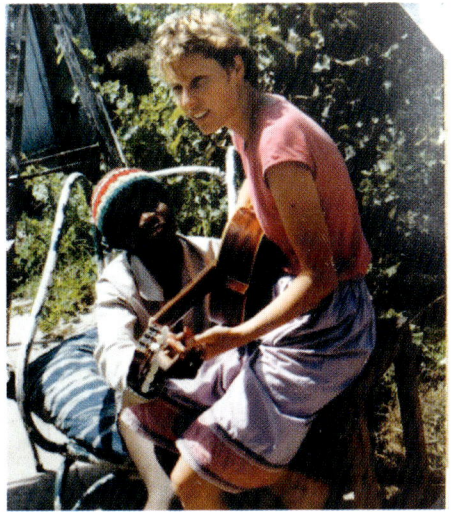

Top Left I am teaching Anne Dolores, a friend from England how to play guitar in Observatory, Cape Town.

Top Right My mother, Mariam Radebe, with supporters at the courthouse during my trial before I was sentenced to go to Robben Island.

Right Middle This is my military uniform from when I was fighting in Angola as a member of Umkhonto we Sizwe (MK), the armed branch of the ANC.

Bottom Left This picture was taken at the entrance of Red Square in Moscow, where I underwent military training before fighting in Angola.

Bottom Right This picture symbolises my throwing a stone against that police Vaillant at that same corner on June 1976.

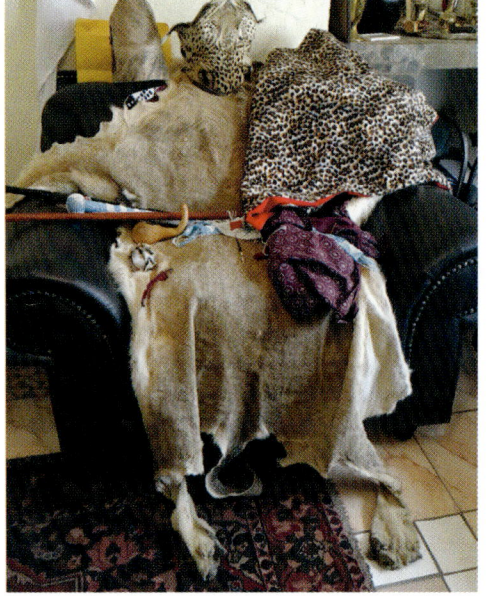

Top Left The co-authors share a moment with friends Thami Ntuli, Melvin Cheasemann and Tsepo Mahlaba after a reading at Wits University in 2016. Photo courtesy of Vukani Cele
Top Right I'm sitting with my wife, Margaret Radebe, during my coronation in November 2015 in Mpumalanga.
Middle This is the part of the ceremony where I kneeled before having oil poured on me to anoint me as king.
Bottom Right During my coronation, I spoke about the need for unity to prevail in Africa.
Bottom Left These are the traditional garments and regalia that I received, which I wear and use while performing my duties as king.

they were not using the skills that they had acquired in the Soviet Union to help liberate the people of South Africa.

'I have a problem because there are many kinds of people from Soweto who are just kept in the camps when we could be fighting a war,' he kept saying. When Steve Tshwete came to us from Robben Island, Nxumalo said to him, 'We need to take off the white gloves and confront the enemy head-on.' Nxumalo was not scared of confronting anyone on any level.

He came to believe that MK's leadership did not really want to wage a serious war against the racist regime. When he was removed from his post of being responsible for infiltrating MK soldiers to South Africa from Swaziland, I took that to mean that the guy's analysis was correct.

'I became a threat because of my involvement in the urban machinery,' he concluded. The urban machinery was those units that created an armed presence in the townships, that would place bombs in cities such as Pretoria and Tshwane. There was also the rural machinery, which operated in areas such as KZN, Mpumalanga and the Eastern Cape. Solomon Mahlangu, the freedom fighter who was hanged at the age of 22 by the regime in 1979, was in the urban machinery. Barney Molokoane, who was a highly effective operative, worked in both the urban and the rural machineries. He was one of three men responsible for the MK bombing of SASOL oil refinery in 1985. The SADF killed him in Piet Retief that same year as he was trying to cross the border into Swaziland.

Nxumalo also developed the theory that the ANC leadership in exile did not want a heavy infiltration of guerrillas to South Africa because it would affect the leaders' families in Botswana, Swaziland and Zambia. A large influx of guerrillas into South Africa would result in the South African government holding the leaders responsible for the guerrillas' actions and retaliating in neighbouring countries where the leaders' families were living.

We saw evidence to support General's idea after Steve Tshwete came out of prison and was made MK's Army Commissar. Tshwete started infiltrating many guerrillas into South Africa. 'The ANC has taken off the white gloves,' the regime concluded. It retaliated in

Zambia, where it started bombing the transit camp called Charleston, and bombed the ANC offices in Harare. As a result, ANC leaders stopped Tshwete from sending more guerrillas into the country.

Nxumalo even engaged the Cubans: 'Help me equip our children to fight an urban warfare.' The questions he raised and the actions he took became too much of a problem for certain ANC leaders: they wanted him out of the way for good. They tried to stop him by labelling him a traitor and accusing him of being sent by the enemy. When that failed, they shot him fifteen times with an AK-47 in Zambia. This was an ANC leader shot by other ANC men!

They left him for dead, but a Zambian man rescued him and took him to a hospital. While he was there, he asked for a police guard because he feared that his would-be assassins would arrive to finish him off. They never came, and he is still alive in Gauteng today.

It was obviously difficult to express your own point of view in this kind of environment. I adapted to it in order to survive. I also used to talk with and conscientise the guys who were prepared to train and fight but were seen as potential mutineers. I told them to change their approach because it was going to land them in trouble.

'Better not ask,' I would advise them. 'Keep quiet and train.'

'I'm being harassed on my base,' they would answer.

'Why did you come here to Angola?' I'd respond.

'I came here to train to free my people,' they always said.

'Then concentrate on that,' I would tell them. 'This place is not your destiny. Your destiny is to free your people.'

Some of the recruits didn't heed my advice, while others could not handle what was going on. At times you would go to the flea market in Kalembe and discover some of your comrades passing through on their way to defect. They would pretend to shop as they aimed for the general direction of the UN headquarters, probably to ask for refugee status once they made it through the doors. Their attempts did not always succeed. The ANC had power with the MPLA (People's Movement for the Liberation of Angola, a Marxist formation); and FAPLA (People's Armed Forces of Liberation of Angola) personnel would bring them back to the ANC rather than allow them to defect. They would then try to defect again, usually via the British and US embassies instead.

Most of the time, they were running away from the harsh conditions in the camp, including the poor food and abuse by our senior personnel. I crossed paths with an MK recruit from KZN who was looking over his shoulder fearfully one day when I was walking back from the Kalembe flea market. He was so desperate to get away that he didn't recognise me. He had only lasted three or four days. We learned after that a man had defected to UN headquarters in Luanda.

You'd see different characters get away, especially if you had underground training. You wouldn't say anything, though. You'd keep it to yourself. You wouldn't be thanked if you reported it: instead you might get arrested and accused of forming a pact with the enemy.

Although defecting was never a possibility for me, I just stood aside when I saw those people attempting it.

KALEMBE AND CONGOLESE were two very big markets in Luanda where you could barter all kind of things. Clothes were often in short supply at the market, however, and Jumbo was the only wholesale store in the country. It was used mostly by the elite because the US dollar was the only currency accepted there at the time. It was more like a diplomatic shop.

The ANC guerrillas had access to used clothes donated by people in Europe. They wore some of the clothes and used others to negotiate with the Angolans for food, liquor and other items. The Angolans at the flea market were often prepared to barter their goods for poor-quality clothing items because of the enormous shortage of clothing in the area.

Angolan women ended up paying dearly for these exchanges. They often didn't have enough money to buy themselves underwear, and some comrades would barter panties and bras for sex. Many marriages in Angola resulted from this activity, and many children were born from relationships that began with bartering sex for underwear. That's how desperate things were for the people there.

MY SIX-MONTH MILITARY training began after we were transferred again, this time to a camp in the east of Angola. Our base was named Matrosov after a Russian soldier from World War II who had used himself as a shield to protect his comrades from being shot and had been killed as a result. The base had also been used by Vincent Tshabalala, an MK soldier who had paid for the fight for freedom with his life. Matrosov was thus a heroic base for fighters and it was an honour to be trained there. It was subsequently renamed after Barney Molokoane.

Vincent Tshabalala was later honoured by having London Road in Alex renamed after him.

WE BELONGED TO THE ground forces and our classes entailed six hours of physical training daily: four hours of running and two hours of exercise. Every day in the camp we would be compelled to run and bark like dogs. Seniors who had already completed their course were the only ones who were allowed to walk. We would stand up for the senior staff and salute them. They would call us 'Kursant', which is the Russian word for army trainees.

Tactics was another intensive course we covered. They would take most of the morning. Sometimes you even had to return in the afternoon. Our training covered both theory and practice. Topography, military combat work, firearm training, urban guerrilla warfare, rural guerrilla warfare, politics and march-and-drill training were other noteworthy aspects of the programme. All in all it was very demanding.

Jefferson, our platoon commander, compounded our difficulties. He constantly worked with his colleagues to make life harder for us, making us run at night without obtaining permission from the camp hierarchy. He argued that he was being tough on us to prepare us effectively to fight for a better world, but in reality he was power-hungry.

He was also envious of anyone who had equal or superior knowledge to him, and disliked intelligent people as a whole. We came into conflict during the part of the training when we were talking about the stages of society and historical materialism.

Jefferson was busy telling us that the first stage was primitive communalism and the second stage was a feudal society. I spoke up. 'Comrade Instructor, the second stage is slavery and the third stage is feudalism,' I said. I offered this contribution based on my background in constructive criticism on Robben Island – not fighting him but trying to help him explain things correctly.

I had been nicknamed 'Lenin' (or sometimes 'Karl Marx') because of my knowledge of political and other topics. Jefferson didn't appreciate my knowledge or my correction of his error. He called off the class and people immediately started to isolate me. Other punishments began soon after that.

Our platoon consisted of 30 people broken into three groups of 10. In effect, when it came to rehearsing simulated attacks, there were 29 other people plus me. I had to carry *all* the ammunition and run at the same pace as the others. Jefferson made me stay on the sidelines when we arrived at the tactical spot we were going to be attacking. Then I had to run back, again carrying the ammo and at the same speed as the rest of the platoon. I don't know exactly what was in Jefferson's mind. This petty and unethical 'punishment' was possibly intended to make sure that I wouldn't be ready for real combat because I had missed out on these military training exercises.

He may have been frustrated with being in exile. I do know for certain that he didn't only hate me. He also loathed an Indian guy whose *nom de guerre* was Izzy Dean. Light-skinned and tall, he had left South Africa as an attorney, and was well versed in Marxism and Leninism.

Jefferson's dislike of Izzy Dean grew alongside his dislike of me. Whenever one of us was punished, the other would be punished too.

Jefferson was not alone in playing these games. Other trainers would push Izzy Dean during our training in urban guerrilla warfare in ways that concerned me.

For one exercise you would have to climb a structure that resembled a building. When you reached what was effectively the third floor, you had to jump to the ground to 'save your life'. Izzy Dean was afraid of jumping, so they would kick him down. 'Indian man, save your life. The enemy is attacking you,' they said insultingly. He landed flat on the front part of his body, limping away as he got up. They spoke to me in the same way when my turn came. 'Black man, jump and save your life.'

On a different occasion, the two of us were thrown into a bunch of red ants. The leaders ordered us to stand at attention while the ants invaded our clothes and bit us left and right. Izzy Dean started tearing off all his clothes when we were finally dismissed. A woman named Vanessa walked by at that point. Izzy Dean didn't care that he was naked because he was preoccupied with removing the ants from his balls.

Then there was the time I wasn't allowed to cross a river over the bridge with the rest of the trainees. Instead, I had to go through the water, avoiding the threat of water snakes and crocodiles. They said that a bridge we were to encounter further on had been mined. It was only for me. There was no minefield for the rest of the platoon. I had again to cross to the other bank by wading through the river.

Lunchtime gave our leaders another, more ordinary way of bullying the two of us. 'Izzy Dean, Sandisile, go and get the pots at the main base,' they would tell us. But when we got to the main base there were no pots to be found. This meant that we had to go all the way back to our own base.

The chefs would dish up the food into large steaming pots filled to the brim with rice or meat. We had to carry these pots using long sticks balanced on both our shoulders, with the kitchen staff positioning them for us. Izzy Dean's greater height made it heavier for me, the shorter one, to carry the pots. Izzy was pigeon-toed and courageous. Even with all the effort involved, we did this without ever complaining.

The abuse began to get to Izzy. He started crying and saying that he wanted to leave Angola and go to London. I did my best to encourage him: 'Don't go back on your commitment. Don't let these people demoralise you. Remember your objective, why you came here. Don't cry. Be strong. Don't give them the joy of knowing that you are feeling the pain they are wishing on you.'

Izzy Dean was able to surmount that moment of intense discouragement and finish his training journey. We developed a powerful energy as a result of our mutual support in the face of the bullying. They tried to break us, but they could not. For instance, despite our learning how to strip weapons faster than anyone else in our platoon, the trainers never acknowledged our mastery of the procedure. They would say: 'No, repeat!' time and time again. Izzy and I would do exactly as asked without showing any signs of annoyance. This was easy for us because we had taught ourselves not to care.

JEFFERSON'S ATTACKS ON me reached a climax during the fifth month. He had already been isolating me from the other comrades by treating me as a traitor. He called me a 'high-profile spy' and invited MK's leadership to the camp for my trial. Chris Hani was there in his role as MK political commissar, together with Mzwai Piliso, the head of intelligence for the ANC and MK. The regional commander and regional commissar of MK were there, as were the camp leadership and all of the trainees and other soldiers. The plan was to try and execute me publicly as an example, to show what happens to traitors.

THIS WAS NOT THE first time I had seen Chris Hani. He used to come regularly from his base in Lusaka to talk with us during our training. We used to refer to him as 'Mister Promise' because he would say the same thing every time he came to address us as soldiers: 'Don't worry, I'm here to identify comrades to fight inside South Africa. I'm here to draw up the list. You are going to go home; you are going to fight. You will all come through Lusaka, where we will deploy you.'

He would make all those promises, but none of those things would happen.

Our leaders seemed happy with the encouragement the commissar of the army gave us recruits. He was there to boost the soldiers' morale, which was very important for people who might be about to be called up. His visits didn't motivate all of us recruits, however. We knew by then that we were by no means all going to go on to fight the regime through force of arms, and felt that Hani's visits were a sham.

The failure of the leadership to deploy most of the trained MK soldiers was plain to see at Matrosov camp. Some people there were becoming desperate to see action.

One guy, Tsepho Wadikapetso, even wrote poems to express his feelings. When Chris Hani visited, Tsepho would write a poem in honour of his visit and recite it in front of him. It would say, 'I am here. I am a fighter. I can fight and defeat the enemy. Don't forget me. Please include me in your list. Give me a weapon. I want to fight.'

Tsepho's words didn't lead to his being called for a long time. But I got to see a different side of Chris Hani on the day of my trial, which gave me insight into why he was so highly regarded.

It was a cloudy day. They gave me a microphone and I stood on a podium in front of everyone. I was nervous about what I knew could happen to me, but I stood by what I had been taught in prison. Unfortunately for the camp leadership, they did not know that I was a prisoner who had returned from Robben Island because they hadn't read my biography. If what I had been taught in prison was wrong, I knew, all those people – Govan Mbeki, Nelson Mandela and the rest – were traitors because they were the ones who had taught me these things, especially Oom Gov.

Chris Hani led the questioning.

'The first question. As you are speaking on the podium, is Angola a socialist country or not?'

'It's aspiring to become a socialist country, but it has not yet reached that stage.'

'How do you understand dialectical materialism?'

I explained the stages of primitive communalism, slavery and feudalism that Jefferson and I had discussed, and which had begun the chain of events that had led me to this point. I described capitalism, imperialism, and the two stages of socialism that Marx and Engels had said countries went through before arriving at a communist society.

'Please do not mind if I ask you another question. How do you see National Socialism?'

'That is what Hitler said he was fighting for, but it was not socialism. It was capitalism.'

'Could you please come forward and whisper your real name to me?' Hani asked me this because we were known in the camps only by our *noms de guerre*.

'Khulu Radebe,' I said quietly into his ear.

'Hey, we've been looking for you! Ramokgadi said you were coming.'

He turned to the rest of the group: 'This meeting is over.'

We went to lunch after that. Chris Hani wanted to know what had been happening in South Africa when we'd left the country and to hear about the Transvaal High Command. Our paths were to cross several times more in the years to come. My situation at the camp improved, as the medical doctor started befriending me and camp personnel edged closer to me.

Since my identity was known, the leaders arranged for me to go to the Soviet Union for further training. I was sent to the Ukraine (then part of the Soviet Union) for about two years. I was in a place called Perevalne in Crimea where many people who were members of liberation movements went for six months' training. After the six months they were often sent for further specialisation in a different camp for a period of at least four months. Some people went to Eastern Bloc countries such as Yugoslavia and East Germany. Others went to different parts of the Soviet Union.

I was part of a group of seven sent from the camps and the frontline areas in Angola to the Soviet Union for training. We were first relocated to Luanda, where we were told to wait until contacted. The leaders did not tell us where we were going, and we only found out about our destination once we were on the plane. Each of us had been living on his own and left on a separate plane. I didn't know any of the other guys at first, but we bonded during the time we spent in the Soviet Union.

Before we started our training in earnest, we attended a Party school to fine-tune our political education. I thought at first that this was part of the intelligence work I would be asked to do. To say I was confused would be an understatement.

Life was rough in the part of the Soviet Union where we did our training. We suffered from the cold and felt suffocated from being indoors all day, every day.

Vladimir was our head instructor. We also had Cubans training us. That's where we learned the Russian words for 'left turn' and 'right turn'. 'Nyet!' they would yell at you if you got it wrong. Instead of 'Forward, march,' they would say, 'March, Shaka'.

They would take us to a pub or two on Friday evenings. I have never drunk alcohol and did not participate. They guarded our group while we drank. One of them would stand up in order to observe us more closely. If they noticed someone downing large quantities of drink, they would make sure to chastise them.

They dealt with people who were drunk by placing them in a simulated combat situation. If everybody was drunk, they set up an emergency combat situation. They would make you run the whole night, until everyone sobered up.

Mostly, we studied. We had a compulsory course in Marxism–Leninism. They also taught us the study of human behaviour. The last course we followed was on military combat work. This covered how to operate in difficult conditions in urban and rural environments. They taught us how to hide weapons, how to drop off clandestine packages at a letterbox, and how to communicate with the local people.

We also did what we called 'military psychology' and a sub-division of military intelligence called 'VIP protection'. Under the latter we covered topics such as how to watch a potential enemy from a distance and how to listen in on enemies and understand their codes. The people who took the course went on to assume officer rank. We wore Soviet officer uniforms when we came back to Angola.

The ANC was connected to the Soviet Union through the SACP. These experiences would not automatically make you a communist, yet you would find yourself delving deep into the philosophy of communism. While we were being taught Marxism–Leninism, we behaved like dedicated communists. Everything we did was communist. That's how we lived.

My life changed again after I returned from the Soviet Union. When I came back to the camp in Angola, my role was that of deputy head of instructors. I taught military combat work, politics, and march and drill. I also continued to practise the behaviour I had learned on Robben Island – basically that of being a good person to those I was responsible for. Little did I know that this would later assist me greatly.

I looked after everybody who was training to become an instructor of political classes. Most of the time, I went to visit the classes they took. That was my main duty. I would look at the teachers' lesson plans and the students' career plans to see if they were headed in the right direction. The students would each come and present their outline to me the next day, and flesh it out throughout the week. I had to listen to their conversations in class to monitor their progress. 'That's fine,' I would tell them when everything was acceptable. 'You are now ready to teach this subject.'

As part of this activity, I was able to evaluate the various new instructors' conduct and level of engagement. I sent the best among them to additional training to specialise.

I NOTICED THAT THE established instructors did not all treat the cadets and new trainees with the necessary respect. You would see them harass their charges. Sometimes I would pull the instructors aside and intervene to say, 'This is not the way. Please treat them with goodwill. They left South Africa to fight in the struggle.'

At some stage, I would end up questioning myself. 'Why did I even come here?' I would ask. My colleagues were neither friendly people nor the kind of comrades I had known and valued. It was a completely different environment from the one I had envisioned. You just kept going for the sake of the struggle and on behalf of the people who were imprisoned for life, not because you experienced comradeship of a rewarding or meaningful kind.

I experienced more threats to my life, too. One day after I had finished training, someone inserted a bullet in my AK-47 when I went to the toilet. I had disassembled my gun and left it with the senior officers as there was an inspection about to happen. There was no bullet in the chamber when I left to pass water. I didn't walk far, just a short distance. Somebody still managed to insert a bullet.

My magazine was on the floor after I'd cleaned my AK, so was nowhere near my gun. As I was standing there holding the gun, I heard a very loud gunshot right next to me. It had come either from my gun or from the gun of someone close by in the room.

My finger was hanging below the knuckle. I allowed myself to be taken to the Cuban doctor in Malanje. They initially wanted to cut my finger off there, and then referred me to the hospital in Luanda because of its better capacity for follow-up treatment. In Luanda, I came across Russian instructors who told me about hospitals in Eastern European countries for more advanced treatment. I never went there. They didn't send me, even after I raised the matter. They just stitched up my finger and it took a long time to heal.

I kept on replaying the event the whole time. Even if there *had* been a bullet in my gun, how had it escaped without me pulling the trigger? The only conclusion possible was that somebody had shot directly at me (and missed a vital organ). But when I asked some of the camp's leaders about holding an inquiry, they said, 'Just forget about it. Move on with your life.' No inquiry was ever held.

Other comrades did not survive the cowardly insertion of bullets in their weapons. And, as with me, the events surrounding the shootings were never properly investigated. They tended to be labelled as suicides. One incident I remember involved a quiet but sharp guy I had trained with who was from the student movement in KZN. He never complained about anything. They told us in the camp that he'd placed his gun barrel under his chin and shot himself on purpose. I question that. I don't believe he did it. This happened around 1986 or 1987 in Barney Molokoane Camp in Malanje. I still cannot make my peace with his death being labelled as a 'suicide'.

I would be lying if I said I knew who had it in for me. My suspicion is that it was guys like Jefferson who had a higher rank than me before I left for the Soviet Union and were below me in rank when I returned. They were supposed to salute me when we passed. I would try to avoid that by telling them they didn't need to.

They again tried everything to ambush me, but unfortunately for them I am not a person one can easily get rid of. Shortly after I arrived back in Luanda, a trumpeter named Welcome Msomi (his *nom de guerre*), whose real name was Themba Mehlomakulu, went to Germany and left me to look after his room.

I got into an argument with a security cluster member named Faku who wanted me to submit the key to him so that an informant he was working with could occupy Msomi's room. The informant was South African and had been working in the deep Northern Front part of Angola. He was married to an Angolan woman and had a child. I reminded Faku that Msomi had asked me, in front of him, to watch the room while he was in Germany. Msomi's room had many musical items and tapes in it, and I didn't want to give the key to a stranger since I was responsible for watching his things.

Faku insisted that the informant with his family be given the room. He then connived against me with the camp commissar, whose name was Sithole and who was deputy head of the Amandla Cultural Ensemble, the musical group I later joined. Pro, the commander of Angola's security cluster, recognised the danger I was in and helped to resolve the issue. He pulled me aside on a street in Luanda to tell me: 'You are a good boy. I like you. I'm sending someone to get the key from you on my orders. Give him the key, because otherwise they are going to kill you.' I felt I could trust Pro's warning about what Faku would do if I didn't give him the key and so gave it to him.

Sithole already had a problem with me because I had brought a saxophonist named Lebogang Mogale into the camp without permission. Unbeknownst to me, he had become involved with Lebogang's wife, Lungi, and had a child with her while Lebogang had been in Tanzania. Lungi was also a musician and had gone to Angola to join Amandla ahead of Lebogang.

Sithole had blocked Lebogang from coming to join Amandla and had made him stay in the transit camp in Viana. I didn't know this and had written an affidavit saying that I would supervise him in the Luanda camp while he played with Amandla during the day and take him back to the transit camp in Viana at night. It took me some time to recognise that Sithole had come to hate me because I had done this. He tried to hide it, but his face revealed the truth.

Driven by this animosity, he acted against me. Despite the fact that I was still a member of the Transvaal High Command and able to make worthwhile contributions on a whole range of issues, I was assigned to work in the kitchen as an assistant cook – for reasons I only came to understand later. I worked there with two guys called Zizi and Fort, who were brought in to capacitate us.

On the day in question, I was with Fort preparing to go and fetch rice in the basement for lunch. It was midday. Suddenly, Sithole's voice erupted in an angry shout.

'Ahh, what are you doing here? Hey! Are you raping?' he screamed. 'Everybody come down, come down, I caught them red-handed, they're raping this woman!'

We had no idea what was going on, until we realised that he was referring to a woman who was sleeping in another room with her husband *and* that he was accusing *us*.

The military police (MP) arrived. The head of the MP was a man whose name was also Lebogang. When he and his colleagues arrived and recognised me, they said: 'No, it can't be this one.' Sithole insisted that we were the culprits and that he had caught us in the act.

So Fort and I were arrested and put into a lead container with small windows that had been cut out using a grinder. They kept us in that container for more than four months. There were other guys there, some of whom had been arrested for petty offences such as smoking marijuana and going out of the camp without prior permission. I would walk around the container so my legs didn't seize up.

In the hot Angolan climate and with those tiny windows, you sweated until you couldn't sweat anymore. They opened the container when they brought food and closed it again immediately after that.

I had no lawyer, I had nobody, and I had four months to think in that container. I had been charged with an offence that was punishable by death. Around the time I was arrested, the son of an ANC leader from the Eastern Cape whose name was Hashe and who had been found guilty of raping a woman, was put up against a wall and shot fifteen times by firing squad. I was told they would do the same thing to me.

If they found me guilty I would be sentenced to death by firing squad just as Hashe had been. Their word was final. I noticed that I was losing weight. At some stage, I gave in to the belief that they were going to kill me.

I got to know some of the other prisoners. Winston, who worked for the ANC, was accused of stealing money. There was Zwelakhe, accused of raping a woman named Jennifer whose husband was with the National Intelligence Service, the apartheid-era intelligence agency. Zwelakhe had contravened MK law by sleeping with the woman. There was a chap arrested for sleeping with a white woman who had been in MK and had run away to hide at the British Embassy in Luanda. We were told that she was a lieutenant in South Africa's Special Branch who had been planted there.

THEY REMOVED ALL OF US from the container at the same time to appear before the military tribunal. You could not see the sun when you emerged. Your eyes were blurry.

We were allowed to mingle with people in Viana camp during the day, but were not permitted to sleep there. We were not supposed to sleep with free people – we were only supposed to sleep with other accused.

We were all transferred to a caravan for our sleeping arrangements. Even though the space was cramped, the mood in the caravan was entirely different. Winston had a small tape recorder and used to play the music of Keith Jarrett. He had a large collection of Jarrett's music. I remember the songs 'My Song' and 'Country', which I liked a lot. It was a whole different vibe, and Winston and I bonded.

WE WERE FINALLY called to appear at the trial. Fort was Accused Number 1 and I was Accused Number 2. The investigation team had a guy named Sishi on it. He had an aunt from Alex named Sis Tlaletsi, whom I knew. We established a connection based on that, and he said that what was happening to us was not fair. He then went to fetch the woman Fort and I were said to have raped.

If the woman testified that we had raped her, we were dead. We were finished.

This woman was from Angola and was a captain in FAPLA. Along with her husband, she played in the military band that performed in the club at the back of the camp. On the day they said we'd raped her, she had been with her husband in the room allocated to them when it had been too late for them to return home after departing late from the club.

'I have been paid to say that this man raped me, but I want to have a clear conscience before G-d,' she said. 'I want to exonerate myself. I don't want to commit a sin in front of this court. How could I have been raped? I was sober and I was sleeping with my husband. My husband was sober. We had come from the club, but neither of us drinks. We had to ask for a place to sleep that night because it was too late to go back to our place.

'How could they have removed my trousers from me?' continued the woman, who was wearing a pair of white trousers as she gave her testimony. 'They were tied. If someone had tried to remove them, I would have felt that. These are innocent people who are being falsely accused. I don't want to have the blood of these people on my hands.'

'How did this rape happen?' she asked the court, pointing at me. 'I've never seen this man in my life. I know Fort, but that does not mean that I was raped by him.'

The court was shocked. Her testimony meant that we were cleared and released. Without it, I would not be here today.

YET WHILE I SURVIVED, the investigating officer who had traced the woman whose words had freed us was found dead in his home several months later. The official reason given for his death was that he had committed suicide. I believe he was murdered because I attended his funeral and witnessed the ghastly way he was buried. I saw the MK officials' hardened faces as they threw his coffin into the grave so forcefully it came apart. 'This is how we bury a traitor who kills himself,' they said in front of his wife, the only family member present.

He was killed because he had not allowed himself to be convinced that we had violated the woman we were accused of raping. He had let us know this and had promised us: 'I'm going to find this woman who is accusing you and speak with her. I've found out that she's a captain in the FAPLA forces.'

Did the people who wanted me dead find out that she was going to speak, pay her, and take revenge on the investigating officer when she told the truth? I suppose I will never know.

I HAD NO TIME to celebrate my victory. Officers were waiting for me when I walked out of court. Commissar Walter threw me an AK-47, a pair of boots and other combat gear. The next morning they put me on a convoy going to the Northern Front to fight against UNITA rebels. We were headed to Paredes, Bengo Province, in the northern part of Angola, where the ANC's military headquarters were located. I could clearly see that these guys still wanted to get rid of me. They allocated me to the first truck of the convoy. If we were ambushed, something which was a near certainty, I was likely to be killed.

When the expected ambush happened, the UNITA rebels unexpectedly shot at the second and third trucks, and I was saved. Still, it was a baptism of fire in the place where I was going to spend the next nine months.

I later concluded that our mistake as MK was to travel all the way from Luanda to the northern part of Angola. Not far from Luanda was the town of Caxito, where we had found a group of civilians in trucks who were afraid to travel on their own because of UNITA. As they had done at other times with other MK convoys, they asked us to cover them so that they could safely reach Quibaxe, a town to the north of Caxito.

We were on the road, with mountains on either side, when the enemy attacked us using what we in the military called a 'balalaika ambush'. This was a double-sided attack, meaning that they opened fire from left and right simultaneously, with bazooka (RPG-7) rocket launchers and AK-47s. It didn't matter which side of the road you tried to drive on, because they had enough men to attack from both sides.

UNITA was a serious opponent that organised its first, second and third echelons to shoot in sequence. The first unit would come up and go full-fire and cease abruptly, at which point the guys in the second unit would stand and blast away. When they had unloaded all their ammo and stepped down, the third unit would pop up and start blasting. In the meantime, Unit 1 would be reloading, followed by Unit 2, and so on.

We heard many unsettling sounds on that battlefield. AK-47s, the weapon of choice for both sides, clattered repeatedly. The RGP-7s that UNITA used issued a long scratchy *whoosh*. The stutter of a Bren light machine gun, originally a Czech gun that had been modified by Britain, occasionally filled the air. UNITA was also known for producing volley fire effects meant to upset your fighting focus. Nothing during our training had prepared the other soldiers on their first mission or me for that auditory onslaught.

Even though MK was glad to help civilians along that long road north, it was a serious tactical mistake. On that terrible day, we were in a line of between five and ten trucks, with eight to ten men on each military truck. We were sheltering the civilian trucks, at front and back, among our own trucks. This resulted in even more limited manoeuvrability for our own vehicles and many MK soldiers being killed by UNITA rebels.

The UNITA forces' trickery also led to our losses. As we were doing our best to respond during the attack, we thought we heard the voices of women hiding in the bush and calling out 'Ajuda' (meaning 'I need help' in Portuguese). But when we went there, thinking that we were going to the aid of civilians, we came under attack from yet more UNITA soldiers.

Those two factors explain, in part, why we lost so many comrades in that battle – and at other times. After the UNITA rebels left, we discovered that we had lost 21 men. There were also many seriously wounded men among the survivors.

Getting our wounded and the rest of us back into the trucks and moving on demanded enormous effort. We had jumped from the trucks to retaliate because we subscribed to the spirit of no surrender. We had survived that attack, but had paid a heavy price.

I was severely demoralised. You're told they're going to kill you in spite of your innocence, you escape, and then are sent to the battlefield to die. It was very bad.

I came to reflect that somehow I'd survived even though we hadn't had a chance. There had to be a God.

Following the ambush we went in hot pursuit of the UNITA rebels in Quibaxe, which was in effect a centre of the Angolan civil war. We were heavily armed. First, we carried ammunition in a bandolier, which took between three and six magazines. We also had what we called a Porsche, a small bag that we placed on our backs, with between four to six magazines. This meant that your upper body was encased in magazines. We also carried an F-1 grenade, and used cello tape to attach two extra mags to our AK-47s.

We were geared for war against soldiers who had a great deal of support from the Reagan administration. A well-organised group, they even had women mercenaries from various Latin American countries supporting them.

UNITA's ambush left no doubt that they were our enemy. We were keen to fight them. But they were very difficult to find, because they were adept at camouflage and guerrilla tactics that kept us off balance.

Moreover, the people who lived in Quibaxe called us *estranhos*, or strangers. We soon discovered that we were dealing with people who had a double identity. One house we came to had a portrait of MPLA leader José Eduardo dos Santos on the wall. You would find Jonas Savimbi on the reverse side when you turned the picture around. People would say they supported the MPLA until UNITA arrived, and vice versa.

We could not fathom at the time why they would side with UNITA. This became clear after we returned to South Africa and General Nxumalo explained to us that UNITA was a legitimate indigenous group formed by the people of Angola. Even though he was born in a Luanda slum, we were told that Dos Santos came from Cape Verde, and that the people had never looked on him as a legitimate representative of their country as a result.

One day a truckload of MK fighters were shot at in broad daylight as they drove past a coffee plantation. Our guys were dead on the truck, but when we asked the workers on the coffee plantation about the murders, they said: 'We were on lunch. We don't know anything.' Most of the people who worked on the coffee plantation were from the southern part of Angola, which was where UNITA was based.

They didn't have ID cards and were not actual coffee plantation workers. They were UNITA rebels posing as workers.

You would keep on searching and looking for these guys, but they would evade you. You might have a *dança*, a dance evening, with the locals because you were trying to develop positive relations with them. Meanwhile, you were dancing with the enemy. They would pump you full of liquor and kill you, and the next day they would say they didn't remember anything.

Sometimes we would be sitting and resting not far from the rebels, and our two groups would end up discovering each other's position. I remember one incident when we ended up a mere 100 metres from the enemy. When they started shooting in our direction, we could hear the bullets zipping past our ears: *zing, zing, zing*. Once we responded, there was a full-on gun battle.

Luckily, I did not die in any of these incidents. Friends of mine were not so fortunate. Some died in front of me. If UNITA defeated you, you usually left your comrades where they had fallen for a certain period as you did not want to hang around afterwards. We would return later to retrieve the bodies and bury them. But in some cases the rebels would chop open the skulls of dead MK soldiers and pour mandioca[4] flour over their brains. This was done to humiliate the dead. They would also undress guys who had been killed, remove all their clothes and leave them naked. Utter degradation.

They didn't do this every time, though. Two MK combatants who were captured by UNITA rebels in the south of Angola told the story of how they had walked from Camalundu to Jamba, UNITA's headquarters. They had trekked day and night with the UNITA rebels, carrying extra bullets in boxes they called *caixas*. When these comrades were asked if they wanted to go back to South Africa and chose instead to go back to the front, UNITA did not treat them badly. We don't know why. That was how it was in Angola. You were always trying to find your bearings.

For example, we would be guarding a bridge over the Rio Cuanza – a tedious task – then going off in hot pursuit of UNITA in very

---

4   Mandioca (cassava) is a staple food on much of the continent, as widely used as mealie meal in South Africa.

hot and humid weather. Struggling to deal with the humid heat of the region, we relished drinking from the cool river and washing ourselves in it.

At other times, we would get stuck in places and suffer from boredom, only to travel great distances at speed within hours. We once marched up to the border with Congo.

While on our own a great deal, we also found ourselves fighting a joint operation in the company of the Katangese, a guerrilla rebel unit that was on MK's side. They were en route from Angola to Katanga, one of the Zaire's eleven provinces at the time. They were skilled at disguising themselves to blend in with the local people.

One day, as we were in convoy with the Katangese going north, we were ambushed by UNITA and one of the Katangese was shot in the genitals. 'Please kill me,' he begged and cried. 'I can't take this pain.' I refused to do it. He died after a few minutes. He was lying on the ground, and then his head suddenly slumped back.

That place was bad in so many ways that you could never fully relax.

To add to the demands made on us, the MPLA and FAPLA forces often ran away from combat. Even though we were experienced in guerrilla training, we regularly found ourselves performing conventional warfare. We were more like an army defending an army acting on behalf of FAPLA.

We provided training for them, too. In Paredes, Bengo Province, we had a base to train guerrillas. This was Pango military camp, which was close to Quibaxe and was meant for crash courses in a variety of skills. A lot of people went there for courses of two, four and six weeks. For instance, left-wing trade unionists would come for two to three weeks to learn how to deal with illicit literature and its distribution, and how to succeed at underground activities such as the placement of limpet mines.

The camp was extremely secret and did not always operate because the area was contested terrain. The Boer regime did not want the courses in Pango to take place, so they would cross the border and destabilise the area. We wouldn't run any courses until they had left.

Although the MPLA and FAPLA forces were paid by the state,

wore uniforms and received subsidies, they were not always able to control the ground and would run away. We, who were not getting anything, would have to hold the terrain. We were doing it for the love of the people of South Africa and for the cause of internationalism. We also took seriously our responsibility of defending the working class of Angola, a socialist-oriented country.

WE HAD NOBLE GOALS, but we battled to eat. I was in Angola for nine months, and there was no food on the front the whole time. Trucks were often unable to reach Quibaxe from Luanda. On the Northern Front, too, there was a shortage of supplies caused largely by UNITA's intercepting them.

We would have to send a unit of between thirty and sixty people to gather bananas. They would go and look for the yellow fruit in the villages further out, at a distance of twenty kilometres or more. They went there with knapsacks and came back loaded with fruit.

The result was that we ate bananas all day. Two for breakfast. Two for lunch. Two for dinner. Besides that, we would get a cup of beans a day. We'd eat the top third of the cup for breakfast; the next third for lunch; and the bottom third for supper. Beans and bananas every day. We also ate rice daily when there was a supply of it. At times, we would have soft porridge.

We often had worms in our food. When you were new, you would remove the worms only to find yourself without any food. When you went for a replacement portion, they would tell you that all the food was finished. So we opted to eat the worms.

We would also be told that no food supply had arrived from Luanda or that the Scandinavian countries had not sent any food in a while. Both statements were probably not true.

Having even some decent food enabled comrades to barter for produce with the locals, thereby increasing the variety of everyone's food intake. No quality food at all meant a more limited diet for everyone.

Yet while all of this was happening, the camp commander and the leadership would be eating tasty meals at the canteen in the administration building. We discovered this when we were told to go and clean the building after they had finished eating one day. On subsequent occasions they would give us permission to eat whatever food was left over, unless they were mad at you for some reason. Sometimes there was leftover fruit cocktail when we went to clean and we made a rush for it.

Whereas the leadership didn't share their quality food, they had no qualms about sending us to do the heavy work of unloading the many weapons that came into Angola from the Soviet Union. These would arrive by sea about once a month. Numerous boxes of bullets for machine guns like AK-47s and PKMs and ammunition for other weapons came, too. I was in charge of offloading them when they arrived in Luanda, a task that took from 10 am until the following day.

There were no breaks. Many people would have to help with the task, including the new recruits. If there were no new recruits available, they would tell people like the musicians in Amandla, who had trained in the 1970s and many of whom were unfit, to go to the docks and offload those incredibly heavy supplies. You had to do it, but you never got paid.

Although the work was heavier than what we had done on Robben Island, we did not think of complaining because we were doing it for the cause of the people and the freedom of South Africa.

We offloaded from the ship onto the trucks. From the trucks, the materials had to be sent to their destination, where another group had to offload them into the stores.

We had to build houses, too. We'd dig a hole in the ground the size of a home for our dwellings, which housed both men and weapons. In other words, we lived below ground and armed. We called the work of building a house 'Operation Moonlight', because we'd work the whole night. Some twenty to thirty of us would be living in the new building and we had to complete it by morning. Logs were needed for the roofing and we had to obtain them by chopping down trees with handaxes in an area outside the camp. We had to carry those trunks back to camp as there were no trucks for the job. I don't remember what type of trees they were, but their weight has remained imprinted on my memory. We had to put up the roofing structure after that. We used corrugated tin and would pour leaves on top of it. This was to stop a passing plane from identifying the house as a military shelter. We tried to make the roof as 'mixed-in' and well camouflaged as possible.

WE HAD TWO DOCTORS. Dr Hagar was black and Dr Bob was white. We also had various medics who had taken a crash course but were not fully qualified. Some had trained in Cuba, others in Luanda. The doctors and paramedics formed a team that was able to deal with a range of ailments. They did exceptionally well with things like malaria treatment. In Angola we had different types of malaria, and they knew how to treat each one.

Sometimes we would march with paramedics, and they would be there with us on the battlefield to bandage our wounds. If someone needed higher-level attention, they would be sent to the medical hospital in Luanda.

There was one incident involving Dr Bob, whose black hair has stuck in my mind. He was the doctor for MK transit at Viana camp. I don't know how he had ended up on the convoy to the north. You did not ask that for fear of being labelled a spy for the enemy and being sent to the Quatro prison camp.

Dr Bob was captured following a fierce battle. When we realised that he was missing, we had to chase after the enemy to grab him from them and return him to where we were. You were dealing with hardened UNITA soldiers from the Northern Front. As they ran ahead of you, they would place their AK-47s back to front on their shoulders and shoot backwards in your direction. For some reason, the rebels had decided to leave him behind rather than kill and undress him, as they did with others. We took Dr Bob back to camp. Not long after that he left for Lusaka, and then for London.

This is just one example of Angola's contradictions and how far our comrades were tried and tested on the battlefield. In one instance, UNITA rebels issued a statement over the radio. 'These MK guys are the best we've come across,' they said. This was followed by an appeal to us: 'Please do not fight us. This is a family war. It has nothing to do with you.' Even with praise of that kind, I felt that we were fighting a losing battle. If it had not been for the Cubans, Savimbi would definitely have won the civil war.

One event that I still don't fully understand haunts me to this day. We were in Paredes, the MK headquarters for the Northern Front, when a convoy arrived. I was there and knew that we were expecting FAPLA forces with vetted commanders. We thought we were receiving allied generals that day, when in fact they were all UNITA rebels.

The rebels came to the headquarters of MK's Northern Front in Paredes. They were dressed in FAPLA uniforms and pretended to be FAPLA commanders and soldiers. Their convoy consisted of a dozen trucks or so.

They introduced themselves to us. We shook hands and embraced one another, but we did not pick up anything untoward. When our leadership got together with the visitors for the planned meeting, they were forthcoming with their information about our plans in both the north and the south of Angola. The rebels asked many questions, saying they wanted a better understanding of the state of affairs. Our leaders briefed them, as one would typically do with comrades.

The visitors left soon after eating the food we had prepared for them.

UNITA DID NOT attack us that day. Instead they used the intelligence we had given them to attack FAPLA forces in a place called Bula Atumba. We later learned that the exact same convoy had taken over Bula Atumba on the evening of their visit to us, killing many FAPLA forces. They had then hoisted the UNITA flag they had brought with them – the one with the chicken logo.

We realised we had been fooled only when some of the people who had survived the Bula Atumba attack arrived at our camp with bloodied and torn clothing the next afternoon. They told us that the convoy that had passed through MK headquarters the previous day had consisted of UNITA rebels.

We were dining with our enemy, but were completely unaware that was the case.

Later we heard that FAPLA forces had been deeply infiltrated by UNITA bandits. They must have been for UNITA to be able to carry out such brazen and successful deceit.

There were many incidents in Angola where you risked your life. Sometimes the danger came from your own people. A case in point was how arrogant some guys were about waking up for sentry duty. One of them, who went by the *nom de guerre* of Mangosuthu even though he was from the Eastern Cape, was extra difficult in this way. Happy to take part in combat, he felt that keeping guard was beneath him. If I had Mangosuthu as my sentry partner, I knew I had four hours of duty ahead of me instead of the two I was supposed to have.

We guarded our positions day and night. One day, I'd been in the post for four hours and my combat gear was soaked through. My boots were uncomfortably damp, and there was no shade where I stood. I got back to our tent and insisted that it was time for Mangosuthu to take up his post. He would not wake up. I left defeated, as I had not yet learned to use the only method guaranteed to rouse him.

On another occasion, I had been guarding the post for three hours as Mangosuthu had again refused to get up. I was upset, but refused to leave the post as this was a highly strategic location. It was one of the entrances to our camp in Paredes, where all the MK kingpins in the war were gathered.

The officer on duty, Thabo, got annoyed. He came to tell me that Mangosuthu did not want to wake up, and concluded with the statement that the best solution to the problem was to wake everyone in the camp. I countered that waking everybody would not help reach our objective. Thabo was adamant. He grabbed his AK and started shooting in the air, right inside the camp. There was no sense in what he was doing.

People in the camp logically concluded they were facing enemy action and started shooting in our direction. Soon, what felt like the whole camp was concentrating its fire on where I was, shooting at me from behind an array of PKMs and AK-47s.

'This is me!' I shouted during a brief pause. 'Thabo was shooting. Cease fire!'

A yell mercifully followed: 'Cease fire, cease fire!'

Then a second, then a third, until silence returned. I was lying on the floor, filthy with concrete powder, while stones fell on me at intervals.

We could have been killed. If I could survive that day, I told myself, I would definitely end up dying of natural causes.

Thabo was sent to dig trenches as a punishment. This did not seem to trouble him, as he'd reached the limit of his patience with guys who refused to get up when it was their turn to guard the camp.

Another comrade with a similar complaint against Mangosuthu took a different approach with him. 'I've got a trick,' he told me. 'Instead of doing what Thabo did, I go in and whisper the sound of an explosion in Mangosuthu's ear, then the sound of a gun – an AK-47.'

'So what happens when you do that?

'Mangosuthu wakes up and says, "Are we fighting now?"'

When the comrade replied that no one was fighting and that he had woken Mangosuthu for sentry duty, he would receive the automatic answer: 'Fuck you. I thought you guys were fighting. You just woke me up for shit. I'm going back to sleep.' The secret on receiving his rude reply was to persist. You simply had to say, firmly, 'No, you're going to the post,' for Mangosuthu to get up from his camp bed and make his way there. Even though the sound of battle was false and came in a whisper, it appeared to be enough for Mangosuthu to perform a task as tedious (to him) as sentry duty.

THERE WERE OTHER humorous moments in Angola. You'd often walk home as part of a platoon consisting entirely of drunken men. In times when we had practically no other food source, we might end up fetching bananas in a village that was some fifty kilometres away, or about the same distance on foot as that between Alexandra and Pretoria. The leaders of the communities we visited supplied the liquor free of charge.

When there was a hill to climb on the return journey, the men would half-fall on the way up and would only stay upright by holding on to their AK-47s. Their heavy rucksacks laden with bananas only increased the sway of their gait.

Comrades would also buy liquor on significant dates such as June 16 to make themselves feel happier about their sacrifices. Because I never drank liquor, I was the one checking to make sure everyone was all right.

When I first told them I didn't drink alcohol, they concocted a foolproof experiment to assess my assertion. After I passed their test, they were satisfied that I would serve them well as a sober guide. They needed someone in the role because, considering the extremely deficient diet most of us received in the camp, any drinking they did was almost always on an empty stomach.

THE REASON I NEVER drank alcohol was that it stopped you from noticing things in life that you needed to be aware of. One time we were at the Intercontinental Hotel in Lusaka, one of the joints where the enemy would send its assassins to check up on the MK leadership. A white Afrikaner policeman followed me, and I evaded him by making a U-turn and disappearing into the toilets. I reminded the guys that the place was flooded with enemy agents. They knew that, but didn't know how to protect themselves.

'Please keep watch for us,' they asked me.

On another day, the men were in camp getting over a drinking binge when the combat bell suddenly sounded. It was part of a test of the camp's readiness for attack. The whole detachment was drunk, from Section 1 to the last.

Chris Hani was there to address the troops. The guys were visibly weaving as he began. They were drunk from maluva, the thick traditional sorghum beer obtained from the palm tree. (In Nigeria, they call it 'palm wine'.) They would obtain it from the locals in the area surrounding the camp. *Kapuka*, a home-made vodka, was another popular drink produced by the surrounding community. The soldiers would often exchange t-shirts or stolen food for the liquor.

One of the guys bumped the guy next to him, who knocked into the next guy, and they all started to fall down. Like dominoes. The commander was so angry that he sent them to the physical training grounds until the liquor was out of their system. They ran the whole night, only becoming sober the next morning. Some of them vomited. The commander showed no mercy. 'What if the enemy had decided to attack us?' he asked repeatedly.

WE WENT THROUGH many adventures in Angola, but what has stayed with me most sharply is the memory of soldiers so young as to be called 'child soldiers'. I still think about them today.

These were young children who were told that when South Africa was free, they would live a life of luxury. They went to the Soviet Union to train and heard about socialism and its wonders. They believed what they were told and sacrificed based on that vision.

When it came to South Africa being free, however, Mandela had a different vision. This vision was not what we, including the child soldiers, had been fighting for.

They never went to school. The slogan they adhered to was 'Liberation first, education afterwards'. What was essential, in their minds, was the freedom of our people. They could think of going to school only when freedom was attained. Only then could it be 'everyone for himself, God for us all'.

But when they came back and looked for work in the 'new South Africa', they were asked, 'What are your qualifications?'

These children, who sacrificed everything to make South Africa a free land, are nowhere in the picture.

They are on the periphery.

They are not invited on 27 April.

They are not given medals.

Their contribution continues to go unrecognised.

They are non-entities – nobody talks about them or acknowledges them.

People say: 'That was then. We should concentrate on the future.'

The leaders' children have had – and continue to have – a place in that future, especially those who received scholarships to institutions in Western countries. They went to America, to Paris and London, and to the Netherlands and Sweden to study.

There has been no place anywhere in South Africa for the child soldiers.

These were children who, in good times, used to eat only condensed milk and cheap tinned meat for weeks on end, and came out with nasty skin reactions as a result. Who were expected to eat soft porridge with worms in it (when there was porridge) and a third of a cup of rice or beans for breakfast, lunch and dinner when there wasn't anything else. Whose only food often consisted of six bananas every day for days on end, two for breakfast, two for lunch and two for dinner. Who had hunger dished up to them, day in, day out. Children who were never offered a means of gaining an education of their choice when this should have been provided to them free of charge. Children who, like me, could not even come home to bury their mother.

What a betrayal. How painful it is.

6
AMANDLA

My time in Amandla began with a jam session we had when Chris Hani came to the Viana camp.

Everything was going well for me. I had returned from the Soviet Union and was the deputy head of the instructors in the camp. I was teaching military combat work, politics, and march and drill. I had a nice office and a Makarov. I was respected. Other members of the military personnel saluted me when I approached them. In other words, I was a highly respected officer.

I knew Chris Hani from my involvement in MK and would have long talks with him about the history of the struggle.

He was a skilled storyteller, but he hadn't come to tell stories that day: he was there to hear music at the jam session.

When a group was performing and they wanted new talent, it was standard for them to ask: 'Is there anyone here who wants to join us?' It would elevate you into something more if you played well.

I had an injured finger from when the bullet in my AK-47 had gone off and I did not want to speak up. Some of my colleagues had a different idea. 'This is your time,' they told me before clapping for me and calling my name. Their pressure got to me, so I climbed up on stage and played.

Later, I blamed myself: 'Why did I go on that stage? Why did I agree to jam that day?'

The guys in Amandla asked me what I wanted to play. 'I'm a

drummer,' I said. 'I can play any style of music.' We settled on playing a song by Weather Report.

Chris Hani listened to what I could do and said, 'This guy must join Amandla.' I went to Luanda, but the other members didn't want me there. They wanted only women in the group, so they could have relationships with them. Having more men would upset that whole process.

They couldn't send me back to Viana camp. Instead they sent me into the kitchen to assist a guy named Zizi to cover their move to thwart Chris Hani's instructions. I was the assistant cook, and would help with the potatoes, the rice and the meat for Amandla's thirty members.

At that time, the group lived in a recreational centre that was full of large rats. I would dish up my food and cover it to eat later when I was hungry, only to discover that the rats had eaten it. Sometimes they ate a lot, up to half of my portion. I would just clean around the part they hadn't eaten and continue eating. At times, there were also lots of ants on the food. I didn't let that stop me, either, and carried on.

I was in that kitchen for months. While working as a cook, I sought permission to assemble a drum kit in the kitchen. My request was granted. I practised every lunchtime because I wanted to be one hundred per cent up to scratch when the opportunity came. I would also listen to music at night with four or five of the Amandla guys I was friendly with after I'd cleaned the pots.

Amandla stayed in Luanda in a suburb called Barrio Popular, but they weren't always around as they went on tour from time to time. I would hang around outside after work with the local kids. They taught me Portuguese.

ONE DAY, AMANDLA director Jonas Gwangwa arrived in Barrio Popular to see how the band was doing. He did not know me or understand that I'd been chosen earlier by Chris Hani to join Amandla.

They were practising a song that the drummer and the percussionist couldn't get right. Gwangwa was becoming frustrated, as he wanted to include the song in Amandla's repertoire.

I was in the kitchen and could hear the noise. The food for the band was almost ready. We used to carry the heavy pots onto the stage while they practised. A queue of people would be waiting with empty plates and we would dish up for them. Zizi would handle the meat, and I would deal with the rice and the gravy.

I walked towards Gwangwa after we'd put down the pots. 'Excuse me, chief. I want to assist these guys to play the song.'

'You are disturbing me,' he said after hearing my voice. 'You're just an ordinary cook. How do you know how to play music?'

'I'm a drummer from SA.'

Gwangwa assented. 'What are you doing?' he asked as I started changing the drums around.

'I'm a left-handed drummer. I need to change the high-hat and the snare drum. I know what I'm doing.'

He also wanted me to count the song for him, because this was his song. 'That's fine,' I said, doing the task to his liking.

We began in earnest, with him counting as well. Before we could finish playing four bars, he stopped and said to the rest of the group, 'How do you put a good drummer like this in the kitchen?'

He was shouting at them and they were looking down at the ground. Their plan had been exposed.

This was gratifying, but I took the attitude that I was to assist the band, not show off my skills. Some guys accepted me fully after that, while others did not. Although the latter group may have been at ease with me when we played, they never truly liked me.

CHRIS HANI AND THE leadership attended an Amandla performance in Luanda a while later. 'Where's *that* guy?' Chris asked, referring to me. By then I was in the field of battle after having been acquitted of rape. My comrades and I were fighting against the regime's 32 Battalion, sometimes nicknamed the Buffalo Battalion, in Angola. We were defending the working class in Angola, or – to be more precise – the country that was owned by the working class and fighting for the freedom of the people of South Africa. We were also defending our ANC camp. I did that for nine months.

The Amandla members answered: 'The guy is fighting in the Angolan bush against the UNITA rebels, so why should he be here?' Because they couldn't properly explain the circumstances under which I'd left for Angola, they were sent to fetch me. I was in Quibaxe in the northern part of the country, where the war was very fierce.

They looked for me, found me and told me that Chris Hani was looking for me: 'Leave with nothing. Don't even take any clothes.'

'No, I don't want to go to Luanda,' I told those guys. 'Tell him I'm fine here.' I said this because I knew I was not welcome in Luanda. They didn't listen. They grabbed me by the neck, tied me up all over and placed me in their V-8 truck. They knew that they couldn't go back without me. That knowledge did not reassure me, as I was still afraid that anything might happen to me on the way back to Luanda.

I was already disorientated from having spent nine months in a war situation in Angola. Beyond that, I had been abducted in a V-8 truck once before. That experience had traumatised me, and the Amandla members were chucking me into another V-8. I was thinking: 'No, they're taking me to the same treatment. I don't want this again in my life.'

Somewhere near the town of Caxito, they stopped the truck and started to loosen my bonds. One guy grabbed me from behind and choked me. This gave the others the opportunity to restrain just my arms and legs, and to pull me back into the truck. Sometime after that, they gave me back my AK-47. Finally, they untied me and drove the last stretch to Luanda.

I ENDED UP SITTING and waiting for a flight at the airport in Luanda, and persisted in asking: 'Where am I going?' They wouldn't tell me, and it was obvious I was getting on their nerves.

I now believed the story that Chris Hani was looking for me and that I was going to meet with Amandla. My international knowledge was minimal at that time. 'Where is this country called Charles de Gaulle?' I asked myself, knowing that I would not get an answer from my captors. 'Only God knows … I'll see later where we're going … I'll ask on the plane,' I told myself.

IN THE MEANTIME, Gwangwa had told Hani, 'You don't need this guy, I need him. I'm taking him to London.' Hani had agreed to this proposal: 'I thought you'd better go with Gwangwa, because I'd heard a bunch of stories. Some of those guys were no good,' he told me later.

I ended up in Paris, not London. I caught a commercial UTA flight straight from Luanda to Paris. Once there I had been instructed to meet Solly Smith, the ANC's chief representative, with whom I would work before going on the road.

I felt totally disorientated when I arrived. My inability to speak a single word of French added to this feeling. I spotted a man who was wearing clothing that resembled an FBI policeman's outfit. He was carrying a placard with my name on it. Should I go towards this coloured man I didn't know?

I started talking agitatedly to myself. 'That man is going to arrest me,' I said. 'That man might be from a special security branch, that man.'

Solly Smith had come to fetch me with his wife and had no idea what I looked like.

I approached him after a while. 'Excuse me, how are you, sir?'

'I'm fine.'

'If I may ask, which direction are you taking?'

'I'm not going anywhere. I'm waiting for someone from the ANC.'

'Hey, man, I'm looking for a lift.'

'I don't know where this guy is. I'm supposed to pick him up, but I don't even know what he looks like. I need to wait for him a bit longer.'

'So are you from the ANC?' he asked after we started talking.

'No, I'm from Zimbabwe.'

'Hmm…'

I'D TOLD HIM I was from Zimbabwe because I didn't know him. Coming from the military psychology school, I knew not to give anything away until I was ready. We kept conversing for a while, and he agreed to give me a lift. I started trusting him as I was chatting to him.

IN THE CAR, I finally told him that I was the person he had come to pick up.

'What's that, man? How can you waste my time?'

'I'm a soldier.'

'Hey, you guys have been messed up over there in Angola. I waited for a long time, you know?'

'How could I trust you? You don't know me, I don't know you.'

'True. I know you are good at military combat work.'

We carried on chatting, and he drove me to the motel where I would be staying for a short while.

FRANCE HAD BEAUTIFUL women. During my first week in Paris, I met a French woman in the reception area of the hotel where I was staying. She had black hair. I couldn't understand a single word she was saying.

She was pointing at her watch and saying '*Quatre*'.

'Hey, I don't understand what *quatre* means, but *quatre* in Portuguese is *quatro*,' I tried to explain.

She pointed at me, stating, 'Me and you, we must meet outside.' I had a full Afro in those days that I used to comb carefully. I was also fit and trim, so found it easy to believe that the woman had instantly taken to me.

We went outside, and she said: 'Me, you, to my home.' Her words set off warning bells within me. 'No, no, no,' I said urgently, experiencing a sudden fright. She might be an enemy agent. If I went to her house, I might end up back in South Africa and inside John Vorster Square. At that time, nothing and no one could ever be trusted.

Interpreting my words as a rejection, the lady with the black hair gave me a well-aimed slap and walked away.

SOMETHING SIMILAR HAPPENED to me a few days after the first slap. A beautiful woman from Guinea came in just as I was going to eat my supper and walked straight to my table. I guess I was the only black person there.

She sat down.
'Hi.' (In French.)
'No, English.'
'Okay, you speak English?'
'Yes, I speak English.'
'Where you from?'
'I'm from Angola.'
'Angolan, English?'
'I'm from Angola, yes. I speak English, but I'm from Angola.'

We started talking. She seemed to like me and suggested going for a walk together.

'No, I can't walk with you in the road, I'm going to be busy in the room now, got some other things to do.'

'Okay.'

I MET HER outside a few hours later.

'You are done now,' she remarked.

'Yes, I've just finished.'

She was with a guy who was wearing a black suit like Mao Zedung used to wear and was carrying a bag. 'I'm going to be killed here,' I said to myself.

'Ma'am, I must be off. I'm in a rush.'

'No, wait, I'm just talking to this man.'

'But I don't understand French.'

'This is my husband,' I heard her telling the man.

'But I'm not your husband.'

'I'm saying that because this guy is bothering me.'

'Why do you use me as your excuse?'

THE MAN LEFT AND we walked together for a while. 'Hey, I must turn back towards the hotel. I don't trust this woman at all,' I said to myself. She walked back to the hotel with me. When we got to the lobby, she left her handbag in my care for a short while. I was worried that there might be a bomb inside.

'Okay,' she said on returning. She took her bag from me and

opened it to place something inside, and I saw that there were a great many French francs in it. (Francs, not euros, were the currency in use at the time.) That was too much money to carry inside a bag, I thought to myself. It might indicate a serious threat.

She entrusted her bag to me again: 'Please take care of my money. I'm coming back, I want to go to the toilet.'

'Why is she not taking her bag to the toilet with her?' I wondered with renewed anxiety.

WE ATE SUPPER together. After the meal, she asked me, 'Will you come to my room?'

'No!' I replied, earning myself my second stinging Parisian slap.

SHE DID NOT WANT to talk to me all the next morning at breakfast. Later that day I asked the guy in our group who spoke English, 'Who is that woman?'

'Why?' he asked.

'She was talking to me last night.'

'She's the daughter of the president of Guinea. She stays here at the hotel. She's at school, studying.'

That was probably why she'd had all that money – her family was extremely rich. I reflected later that she may have been completely straight with me. Still, there was no way I could afford to take the chance.

MY WORK IN FRANCE first entailed assisting in the office and engaging with NGOs and the anti-apartheid movement. That assignment didn't last long, and I soon joined Amandla on its travels all over the world.

Amandla was created after the ANC identified four pillars of the anti-apartheid struggle at the Morogoro Conference in Tanzania in 1969. The pillars were mass mobilisation; underground activity; the armed struggle; and international mobilisation of the anti-apartheid movement. I ended up participating in all of them.

Amandla's formation was a core part of the effort to mobilise the international community in the fight against apartheid. It had begun in 1978, following the participation of a contingent of ANC youths at the World Youth and Student Festival held in Cuba. It was decided that the group should be continued to showcase South African culture and do battle with the racist regime.

OR Tambo was a founding member of the Amandla Cultural Ensemble who personally conducted the song that accompanied the traditional gumboot dance. 'In our country, a new social and political order is being born,' he said in 1985. 'Our artists have to play an ever-bigger role in participating in the creation of this glorious future. Let the arts be one of the many means we use to cultivate revolt and inspire millions to fight for the South Africa we envisage.'

Eventually, Amandla consisted of a cast of about thirty people who excelled in different artistic genres. The performance, which would take between one hour forty-five minutes to two hours, was part of the Release Mandela Campaign. We musicians sometimes filled other roles, especially when a cast member was sick.

Jonas Gwangwa coordinated the whole programme. We would use music, song (including a cappella), dance, traditional instruments, poetry and narration to take the audience on a journey through South African history and to illustrate our vision of the South Africa we were trying to build. We wanted to bring to the world the sufferings of our people and the kind of South Africa we envisioned, and to do this by demonstrating our humanity, traditions and culture rather than portraying our victimhood.

The performance began with an image of how South Africa had been before colonialism. It depicted a young unmarried woman wearing traditional clothing and going to the river with a jug to collect water. A chap then arrived on the scene to propose to her. She agreed to be his wife by performing the traditional gesture of giving him one of her beads.

The next scene showed a king seated somewhere in South Africa and being visited by colonialists who wanted to talk to him. They had brought him presents. The king was happy with the gifts before the colonialists started expecting the indigenous people to obey their form of governance and forced them into slavery. They took away their land and imposed taxes on them, and the people were forced to go to the mines as workers.

Next came a portrayal of the development of cities, with people queuing for transport to take them to work. A young chap at a taxi rank was shown cleaning shoes for people who had not had the time to do this before going to work early in the morning. The boy was being paid for his work but, because of the system of capitalism that had been created, people were motivated to steal or even to kill. Thieves appeared while people stood in the queue and started pickpocketing.

The young chap ended up dead. A poem was recited as he was carried off stage, which was a tribute to him and an indictment of the system. It spoke of him as 'a victim of the hungry wolves', a clear reference to capitalism's brutality and cruelty.

After that scene came a depiction of the emergence of the struggle in the urban areas. Nelson Mandela was shown emerging as a leader in the 1940s. This was followed by the Defiance Campaign of the 1950s. The formation of Umkhonto we Sizwe (MK), the 'Spear of the Nation', came after the banning of the ANC in 1960. We also showed the Rivonia Trial, where Mandela, Sisulu, Kathrada and the other defendants were sentenced to life in prison. We recited a statement from the MK Manifesto:

> The time comes in the life of any nation when there remain only two choices: submit or fight. That time has now come to South Africa. We shall not submit and we have no choice but to hit back by all means within our power in defence of our people, our future and our freedom.

From there, the audience was able to reflect on the trial of Nelson Mandela. Before the first half of the programme came to an end we recited his stirring statement from that trial: 'I have cherished the ideal of a democratic and free society... It is an ideal which I hope to live for and to achieve. But if needs be, it is an ideal for which I am prepared to die.'

The programme shifted to a more contemporary focus after the intermission. For Act II we brought in individual singers, one of whom was Sis Esther. Another one – whose name was Jennifer – we nicknamed 'Golden Voice' because of her rich, almost tenor-like voice. We also had two guys, Santana and Mbongeni, who sang a traditional Zulu song about the unity of the struggle in fighting the regime.

One of our most dramatic performances was that of the gumboot dance, the iconic rhythmic dance developed by miners in South Africa, during which the dancers create a unique sound by slapping their hands against their boots and parts of their bodies. Dressed in gumboots and overalls, the miners on our stage were shown digging trenches, breaking rock with pickaxes, and getting together to share their experiences and relax after working a demanding shift underground.

After the dance, two men representing workers in general would come onto the stage. The first was injured and supported by the other. They came up to the microphone and sang about the depth of the pain that came with being a worker in South Africa.

The focus on workers was followed by a slot dedicated to the student uprising of June 16 1976, in which we conveyed the events of that time. This was a slot in which I participated as more than just a musician.

We had a medley at the end of the show. We reflected on Mandela and other prisoners and called for their release from prison as part of the Release Mandela Campaign. As a finale, we would have a sangoma as a symbol of African tradition and all of the indigenous nations showing off their different traditional dances. We had a Pedi dance, a Shangani dance, a Sotho dance, a Tsonga dance, a Xhosa dance, and others to express South Africa's great diversity and cultural wealth. There was also a Venda celebratory warrior dance, of the kind performed when men came back victorious from battle. We would close with a dramatic Zulu dance, during which many in the audience would be amazed by how high the women could kick up their legs.

As we danced, we sang these lyrics:

'This is our war.
It's only meant for those who are tried and tested.
Those who are brave must go in front.
Those who are afraid to confront the enemy, go back.
Give way to those who are tried and tested.'

EVERYBODY WOULD BE impressed and happy by the end of the show. A lot of white women would come after you because they thought of you as a warrior.

Although the music we played remained more or less the same from show to show, we adjusted the content to reflect recent events in South Africa and the state of activism in the country. We were supposed to be 100 per cent informed at all times about events in South Africa, and our script had to reflect the latest reality. The ANC would send us up-to-date information, which we would incorporate into the show. After 1983, for example, we started displaying UDF posters in the course of our shows.

We would engage intensely with the audience after the show. After we'd performed, we would quickly go and change before meeting with them. The commander, the commissar and selected members of the Executive Committee would speak to the audience. (The Excom at the time might include a person who'd left South Africa recently and could speak about matters there with greater authority.) We'd also have private interviews, during which we were able to talk in detail with journalists. Our performance was celebrated with flowers and interacting with the audience and with journalists before going for dinner.

I was elevated to the role of head of protocol shortly after I joined Amandla properly. This put me on the Executive Committee and included my serving under the security cluster of the ANC, which was called the Department of Intelligence and Security (DIS).

Being responsible for protocol meant dealing with issues like passports for group members. I would deal with tickets and talk to the officials whenever we went to an airport. My role led me to be despised by some of the guys in the group. Taylor, a member of the cast with a bald head who often played a white soldier, even told the commander that I had to be a policeman. 'How else did he go from not being part of the group to being on the Exec as the head of protocol?' he would ask.

WHENEVER THERE WAS an argument, the airport officials would ask who the head of protocol was and I would inevitably respond with: 'What seems to be the problem?' I would have to sort out any issues that arose and would also take the rap if people weren't acting right.

This happened a number of times. On one occasion, we landed in China to transit to Japan. We had a connection time of thirteen hours. The Chinese officials asked us to submit our passports and gave us official paper passes in exchange that allowed us to go to town. The policy was that you would return that piece of paper to the authorities to get your passport back from them.

Unfortunately, some of the guys were drunk when they came back, and one of them had lost his pass. It was clear that I would have to talk with the migration officers.

They were annoyed. Referring to the member who had lost his pass, a man named Papa, they told us: 'Your colleague did not bring back the paper. No paper, no passport.'

We all had Ghanaian diplomatic passports, which that country's government had donated to enable us to move around the world. We needed to present them at that moment to travel to Japan. I tried to negotiate. 'Man, my apologies,' I said. 'My sincere apologies. Please have mercy on him.' We were speaking with the officials in English, which did not make things any easier.

'Who are you?' they asked.

'I'm the head of protocol,' I responded.

'You are heading such disorganised people.' They were looking at me very seriously as they said this. I'd never seen people as serious as those.

'Can we see your passport?' they asked.

I had already retrieved my passport and I resubmitted it to them.

They held on to it and told me, 'We are punishing you for travelling with disorganised people.'

I REALISED AFTERWARD that this had been a tactic to punish me for just a few minutes. But it didn't feel like it then, when a still drunk Papa got into a confrontation with the main Chinese official. Walking straight up to him, he called him a motherfucker in Sesotho.

The official was standing there stiffly. 'What is this man saying about me?' he asked.

'He's not saying anything bad,' I lied while trying to get Papa away from the official without success.

'Are you defending this man?' the official exclaimed. 'I don't understand the language, but I can see from his expression that he is swearing at me.'

At this point, Jonas Gwangwa came into sight. Because he was Amandla's director, I thought that he might intervene with the drunk guy. I tried to tell him, 'I'm having a problem here.' He gave me an expression as if to say, 'It's not my problem,' and walked straight past me and towards the plane.

I knew that I couldn't leave Papa behind: he was my responsibility and I would be locked up upon my return. 'Why did you leave this man in Beijing?' the leaders would ask me.

Another Chinese official arrived at this point. He had a separate complaint about Jennifer, an Amandla member who had also lost her piece of paper during the trip into town. She wasn't drunk, but she had lost it nevertheless.

While I was busy dealing with these two complaints, a third one landed in my lap. Another drunk member, this time Taylor. I was still handling Papa, who had continued to swear at the guy who was head of migration. He kept telling him to go to hell.

I told him, 'Please stop insulting this man. We want to go to Japan. You are delaying us.'

The official turned and walked away with my passport.

I was left with Papa, Jennifer and Taylor. People were boarding the whole time this was happening. After a while, we concluded that the plane must have taken off for Narita Airport in Tokyo.

'Papa, you messed it up,' I told him. 'Let's bargain for another connection.' After a long half-hour, the official returned and said: 'I'm giving you forms, including you. You just have to fill them in, then I will release your passports.'

Papa was still drunk, Taylor was still drunk. But the official returned and gave us the forms on which to fill out our information. Our path seemed clear.

Jennifer and I got busy, and Papa and Taylor seemed to be coping. But on closer inspection, where the form said 'Male,' Papa and Taylor had both ticked 'Female'.

I begged the man for mercy, and he ultimately gave us the passports. Papa kept insulting him, over and over again, until we climbed into the plane, which had been seriously delayed. Unbelievably, we had made it to the next step of our journey.

ANOTHER ALCOHOL-RELATED incident happened when we were flying from Zimbabwe to Tokyo, via Addis and Beijing. Once in Addis and thanks to those diplomatic passports, we were allowed into the VIP lounge and began to relax.

Suddenly, police were everywhere in the lounge. Heavily armed men surrounded us.

Little had we known that one member of our group, Charlie, had downed whiskeys on the plane from Zimbabwe and had been completely drunk for a while. It was thanks to him that we were being encircled by police.

He had told a person he was talking to at some point that he was with a group of terrorists from South Africa who were proceeding to Japan. He had meant to say 'freedom fighters', but had said 'terrorists' instead. On being told of Charlie's proud announcement, the head of migration had advised the police of the presence of a group of terrorists in the VIP lounge.

I stood up because I was the head of protocol. A man told me sternly to sit down.

'I want to clarify one point,' I said from a sitting position. 'Where did you get this information?'

They pointed at Charlie.

I explained that we were a group of South Africans who were fighting against apartheid. Looking relieved, they put down their guns. 'We are under siege from terrorists,' they said, then let us go.

THREE OF US faced real danger in Belgium.

We were taking a walk around Brussels when we noticed a white guy tailing us. 'There's a guy following us,' one of us said shortly. We had all noticed him at more or less the same time, as you had to be a trained soldier to become a member of Amandla.

We kept him in sight by using the reflection off the windows behind us, then moved to the opposite pavement. He did the same. While we were trying to verify our suspicions and cut the tail, we moved pavements again. So did he, at which point we picked up our pace.

We then went into a shop and told them that there was a guy following us who wanted to kill us. They called the police and the guy disappeared. We never found out who he was working for, but we remained convinced that he had wanted to do away with us.

WE HAD OTHER unsettling experiences with other ANC members that were not as scary as that one. One of them occurred when we were touring Australia, where the chief of the ANC Mission was Eddie Funde, the prominent South African who became ambassador to Germany in 2008.

I was with Lebogang and some of the other guys one day. Hungry and without money for food, we decided to pay Funde a visit.

He told us that he had no money for us. We kept engaging with him as we suspected that he was not telling the truth. He was wearing a jacket and kept his hands in his pockets the whole time he was talking with us. We didn't realise, at the time, that those hands were holding Australian dollars. Many of them.

As we persisted, Funde became angry with us and started to threaten us. He took his hand out of his pocket to wave his finger at us. A roll of money fell out as he did this.

Funde tried to put his foot on the fallen money, and lifted his hand out of his other pocket in an effort to retain his balance. Another roll of banknotes hit the floor. He placed his other foot on that.

He started to laugh, then asked, 'How much money do you want?'

'We don't want it,' we replied. 'Since you've been telling us there is no money for us while carrying so much cash, we'll go look somewhere else.'

PLAYING AND INTERACTING with other cultural groups was a major part of our work in Amandla. In 1987, a symposium coordinated by the ANC gathered together a large number of organisations drawn in large part from the Mass Democratic Movement. Many of the delegates who attended were aligned with the UDF. Musicians and progressive artists who were part of the Cultural Resistance Movement were also represented.

We met under the theme of 'Culture in Another South Africa'. There was already a pretty widespread belief at the time that there *was* going to be a new South Africa; so we met to discuss the type of culture we wanted to belong to within the country. How best to fuse the nation's many traditions and traditional ways of life with Western ways was a strong concern.

A band called A Re Kopaneng (Let us unite!) was put together for the occasion. All South African musicians, notably those who were in exile, were invited to play together, as the band was based in England and Sweden most of the time.

Although we had agreed that we would play only South African music and that we would play all the chosen songs together, Abdullah Ibrahim insisted on playing solo. I don't know why he wanted to do this when the whole point was to come together.

This was a big gathering in a concert venue that could hold hundreds of people. Despite coming from different quarters, all of us had made it there in time. Together, the rest of the South African contingent decided: 'You know what? Let him go to hell. We'll perform his songs too, in fact we'll start with his songs. We'll finish them all, then move on to the rest of the programme.' Abdullah Ibrahim cried when he arrived. He was extremely angry because he could hear his music being played by people other than himself.

Hugh Masekela was in the line of fire too.

I liked Bra Hugh. We are relatives since we both belong to the Hlubi clan. If you listen to recordings of Bra Hugh's music, you will notice certain notes he liked to play around with. He was very free with those. As we were practising the marabi piece we'd be performing alongside him, we held a short, whispered discussion that ended with a mischievous suggestion: 'Let's change the chords.

Let's go up one level.'

Most marabi music is situated within three or four chords. But that day we transitioned to an upper note that Bra Hugh was not used to playing and was therefore unable to reach. We did this to him in the middle of a solo. He had to wait until the transition was over to start playing again.

'Stay there, don't come down,' we teased him.

He was angry with us, even though we'd done it just for fun.

Bra Hugh's theme song was 'Grazing in the Grass'. He loved, loved, loved that song. It was without a doubt the favourite song of his entire artistic career. We initially nicknamed him 'Grazing in the Grass' because of his love for the song, not because he liked to eat.

'We must play "Grazing",' he would say during any discussion of a forthcoming programme. So everybody ended up calling him 'Grazing'. He was initially mad about that, too, but got over it in later years.

All in all, Amandla visited more than forty-five countries. We went to African nations such as Ghana, Nigeria and Zimbabwe, and to the Middle East and Israel. We went to Asian countries such as Singapore and Malaysia, to Latin American countries such as Brazil and Cuba, and to the United States and Canada in North America.

The countries were selected on their potential to mobilise support for the anti-apartheid movement. Before OR Tambo visited a country, they would send us there to prepare the ground for him. New Zealand was one example of how useful this approach could be. It rejected us at first: we were met by protesters wearing tyres around their necks in reference to necklacing and opposing our presence. After engaging with us, they changed their view and welcomed OR to their community. After seeing an Amandla show in London, Tambo said that it took him twenty years to do what Amandla did in two hours – to promote South Africa and the struggle for freedom – according to the South African government. We were the people who cleared political obstacles for him.

Amandla remained in Japan for almost three months in 1990. The people there were welcoming and supportive of our cause. I mastered the art of holding chopsticks there after being told that it was compulsory.

We started mingling and creating friendships and toured the

whole of Japan. We performed in Hiroshima and Tokyo and went to other areas such as Osaka.

Mandela was in Osaka at the same time we were. The ANC had been unbanned, he had been released and he was out raising money for his beloved organisation. Mandela, or Madiba as everyone had started to call him, was so joyous that he came up onto the stage and danced during the performance.

Meeting him in Japan was a surprise. We had already met twice after his release. The first time was when I was coming off a flight at the airport in Paris as part of my work for Amandla. 'Hey, are you here?' he asked as he caught sight of me. The last time I had seen him before that moment was as a prisoner on Robben Island. Winnie was with him in Paris. She too was surprised and pleased to reconnect as we had worked together in Alex. The second time was during his first visit to Angola. I was on vacation from Amandla in Paris and had gone to Angola. The diplomats there asked me to serve in the guard of honour put together to welcome him. I told the guy who asked me that I was not a diplomat. He insisted that we 'didn't have time for that'. Nelson and Winnie were again together, and smiled at seeing me in the line.

THE BLUNT AND unexpected message we received from the ANC straight after the concert and joyous reunion was anything but friendly. 'You are on your own now,' ANC treasurer Thomas Nkobi told Amandla, in essence. 'The ANC has done enough for you. Don't expect anything else from us.'

We didn't understand why he was saying that right then, but we soon learned that the message he had delivered was true.

7
RETURNING TO SOUTH AFRICA

In 1990, following the unbanning of the ANC, the Home Affairs department in South Africa gave me just one month to return to South Africa. I came home within the stipulated time and soon discovered that I was still persona non grata.

The police found me on 3rd Avenue in Alex and pointed guns at me. They told me that I was being arrested because they believed I did not have permission to be in South Africa. They had overlooked that I had applied for indemnity through the ANC legal office under Lindiwe Sisulu.

I was in fact returning from a visit to Luthuli House in Johannesburg with the necessary permit in my pocket and was able to show it to the police. I was then allowed to be home, and my comrades gave me a welcome party. Dr Wally Serote, who later served as South Africa's poet laureate; Justice Hlomuka Ngidi, who became mayor of Sandton; Joe Manana; and Welile Nhlapo, posted to the United States as South Africa's ambassador in 2007, were among the people who celebrated my return.

Then the Special Branch visited me.

They found me playing my drums. I had closed my eyes as I played and they waited for me to finish the song and open them. I wanted to rewind the song when I did. There were anywhere from sixty to a hundred of them. Some of them were sitting. Some of them were standing. They were all having a free concert.

One of them picked up my sticks, but the guy in charge – the head of the Special Branch – interrupted him and said in Afrikaans: 'This is not a terrorist. Let's go. The guy is a professional musician.'

Even though they left right away, I found it impossible to continue with my music. You open your eyes and find the Special Branch pointing multiple guns at you. I was no longer sufficiently at peace to play.

I took a break for a while.

Fortunately, I was soon saved from my musical exile by a reunion with the members of Roots, the band I had belonged to on Robben Island. Things improved after that.

THE ANC HAD a long tradition of cultural struggle. In the early 1970s, a branch of the liberation movement was formed for the many artists who were not being recognised for their important role in the struggle. The ANC in exile had an Arts and Culture Department headquartered in Lusaka and led by Barbara Masekela, Hugh Masekela's sister. We used to call it the DAC. You would find writers, poets and musicians under that department. Artists living in exile in the liberation camps were encouraged to group themselves under various cultural categories whenever there was a significant ANC national day like Freedom Charter Day.

In 1982 the DAC staged a cultural symposium in Gaborone, where the decision was taken to use culture to intensify the struggle. There was another symposium in 1987 in Holland, which posed the question: 'What kind of culture do we want to have?'

MK MEMBERS WHO were musicians and were caught after leaving Angola to perform missions in South Africa would often meet and play together in prison on Robben Island. These activities coalesced into a band by the name of Roots. The music was based on the struggle and the lyrics were political. We would practise on weekends because we didn't work on Saturday or Sunday. The international community donated our instruments.

I was the drummer. The lead singer was Ronnie Mabena, and the second-in-charge was David 'Shuffle' Jwara. We had a lead guitarist named Curtis Mhlanga and a bass player named Dobler. On rhythm guitar we had Frank Thabane, whom we called 'Machini' (Machine). We also had a horn section, in the form of an alto saxophone, a bass saxophone, a trumpet and a trombone.

AFTER THE UNBANNING of the ANC and other liberation movements, the idea came to us to revive Roots. 'We are now all on the outside,' we said. 'Let's get together again.'

I was appointed musical director of Roots. The experience I had gained in exile through Welcome Mehlomakhulu, Bheki Mseleku and Jonas Gwangwa had enhanced my talents as a musical director. I tested those skills and my abilities as a music arranger while playing with Roots for a second time. I arranged and rearranged all of Roots's music, making it a little more advanced. I didn't tamper with the music, just added a fusion flavour to it.

We had ample time for the band when we first came back. As former prisoners, we used to meet at the same Dorkay House my Aunt Ntombi had said she would take me to as a child. We were given our venue by Queeneth Ndaba, who told us that the centre was all about supporting township music. Dorkay House had remained a site of support for many popular township musicians, such as the African Jazz Pioneers, Kippie Moeketsi and the Dark City Sisters. We all performed gigs for the ANC to conscientise people through music.

Roots performed at my wedding. The day I got married, I came two hours late to the wedding after a gig with them. We arrived back in Alex at 2 pm. I quickly changed into a suit at my place and we drove to my wife's home on 10th Avenue. I danced a little in the street, as South African tradition required, while the women ululated. After we returned to my wife's yard, I switched and started performing as part of the band.

I actually played in two bands. One was with Jonas Gwangwa. The group had not received much support from the ANC following its return to South Africa, so Gwangwa had formed another band. Roots was the best band I ever performed with. Everybody was in the vibe and we just moved into the experience as ex-prisoners who shared a past. We played around South Africa when we came out, and the public everywhere took to our music and our band. Roots was equal to famous bands like Sakhile and Bayete. Groups who were famous for playing Afro-traditional music grew scared of us. Our song 'Sicelo' became the number one song on Metro FM for more than a month, and featured in the top ten nationally.

In 1991 we were invited to the 'Children of Africa' concert in Lagos, Nigeria, and commissioned to play three songs. We met popular African artists like Osibisa and even played with Rita Marley and the Wailers. The Wailers played first and then we took the stage. Now *we* were accompanying Rita Marley, Bob Marley's wife.

Hugh Masekela listened to us and said, 'You guys are lying. You are not prisoners.'

We told him that all of us had been on Robben Island.

'Never, never in my life have I come across this music from prisoners,' he yelled. 'You motherfuckers are going to play *six* songs, not three!'

After we finished playing, Rita Marley, Osibisa, Third World, King Sunny Adé and a couple of other international musicians took all my sticks as souvenirs because I was the only left-handed drummer they had ever come across. Everyone wanted to watch me perform and to take my sticks afterwards as a souvenir.

I left Nigeria with only my brushes.

IN ADDITION TO PLAYING gigs, we recorded a CD in 1991 that holds up well more than thirty years later. It shows what skills I had inherited from Bheki Mseleku and other jazz giants.

The CD features nine songs. One of them talks about 'giving a thought for Africa'. Another one says, 'We were rich before the white man came to Africa. We had kings, we had houses, we had land, we had cattle, but now we are dehumanised. We are trusting you, the little ones, to restore dignity and respect among our people and our nation.' A third song refers to a missing boy. It asks, 'Who has seen the little boy who disappeared last night when we were sleeping?' It follows this by stating that 'Africa is crying because a little boy is missing from the nation,' and goes on to name some of the murdered heroes of the struggle: 'Where is Hector Pieterson? Where is Solomon Mahlangu?' A fourth song laments how far we are from home. 'We are in exile,' it says. 'When we go home, we must look for the graves of our forefathers because they were buried while we were away.'

One of the most powerful songs is about a Xhosa-speaking person who seeks greener pastures in Gauteng before deciding to leave owing to black-on-black violence.

IN ALEX, THE VIOLENCE started on a beautiful Saturday morning, when men were bused in from different hostels outside the township into Alexandra stadium. You could see many buses and taxis coming into the stadium and making it their assembly point. The Afrikaner police drove into the stadium with an arms cache in a white kombi. The taxis and the hostel dwellers started spreading out and killing people shortly after that.

We knew that this type of violence had already started in Natal. They wanted to get rid of all of the Xhosas and so get rid of the ANC. 'We don't have any problem with any Zulus, but we want to get rid of the Xhosas because they are ANC.' That's what these guys had been told. That was when we'd realised that the National Party and De Klerk were in cahoots with the Inkatha Freedom Party (IFP).

MY FRIEND KEIKO, who was from Japan, had slept over the night before and ended up witnessing one or two of the killings that ensued. I knew that we had to get her out of Alex as soon as I saw the men gathering at the stadium. Even though I didn't own a car to move her, I knew that Keiko had to go.

My wife and I had to handle this situation. If we had to die, we had to die, we decided. In addition to Keiko being our friend, there would be an outcry from Japan if she was killed. I eventually managed to arrange for her to stay with Andrew Mlangeni, the Rivonia Trial defendant.

A CHAIN OF SHACKS stood close to our house. Most of the occupants were Xhosa people, and the hostel dwellers started by murdering them. We saw it happening. They shot people. They even shot one of their own. There was blood everywhere. They mostly killed men, but murdered women, too.

At various times that day a taxi came into Alex, pretending to be taking people to town and moving around the township looking for customers. Once the taxi was packed, it was driven to the hostel. Everyone was killed, even children. The driver was one of the killers.

They killed a woman with a baby on her back on the stoep of my wife's house. The baby survived the attack, but was left screaming on top of her dead mother. They also murdered a man who was approaching the house. My wife had to hide and keep silent because they would have come for her if the man had seen her and called for help. To this day, she does not want to go to that part of the community. She is too traumatised by the memories of what she saw and heard.

THESE DEVELOPMENTS WERE not totally surprising to me. When we'd travelled to Japan with Amandla, we'd seen a group of young people from Natal who were on their way to Israel for military training. This was during the time when South Africa and Israel had a close connection. We'd met them at the airport in Addis Ababa, Ethiopia, and had learned what they were going to be doing in Israel while chatting to them in isiZulu. We started engaging with their leader, who was not forthcoming. We overheard him shouting harshly at the youths for the mistake they had made in sharing that information with us.

I suspected that these same young boys were among those being dispatched to hostels to target Xhosa-speaking people.

MANY OF THE ORIGINAL hostel dwellers in Alex were amaPedi people from Limpopo and amaBhaca people with their roots in the Eastern Cape. They worked for the Sandton Town Council and a milk-processing plant close by. There were also some Masinga from the abaThembu clan in the region of Msinga in KwaZulu-Natal, whose adults pierced their earlobes and wore ornamental earplugs. They never joined in the killings as they do not consider themselves to be part of the Zulu nation or the Zulu Kingdom. In other words, the lawful occupants of the hostel did not include any Zulus.

On that Saturday morning, these rightful hostel dwellers had to relocate while the killers moved in.

THE POLICE THREW UP a razor-wire barrier around Alex that had the effect of locking everyone inside with the IFP. We watched events unfold through the window.

The attackers had information about who among the community supported the ANC. People had joined the Congress in big numbers after its unbanning in 1990. By then, my wife was a well-known office-bearer with the ANC Women's League.

When my wife ventured out of the house she encountered groups of Zulu people from Alex marching along and chanting warrior songs. Some of them would greet her quietly so that no one should be aware that they knew her. 'We are not in Inkatha, but we are forced by the conditions to take part in these marches,' they would tell her.

It was clear that conflict had been imported into Alex. Many people were bused into Alexandra and dropped off at the stadium. They used to sleep there, then go out to kill people in the township. The Inkatha leaders and members, who had commandeered semi-permanent space in the Madala Hostel by kicking out most of the traditional amaPedi and amaBhaca occupants, were also involved in the killings.

BEING ENCIRCLED BY the enemy was suffocating. You felt as if you couldn't breathe properly the whole time. You couldn't say, 'Let's run away.' The Afrikaner police stood on the other side of the fence, and the only time they would open it was to bring in more arms for Inkatha. It was a situation of basic survival.

I had come home to a war zone that was more tense than growing up under apartheid, serving time on Robben Island, or surviving in Angola. We slept and ate in the same area as the killers. It was so bad that people named the area 'Beirut'.

We eventually came to a clearer understanding of what was happening. Even though the term 'black-on-black violence' was used to describe the situation, the true origin of the murders was that the racist regime in South Africa had found parties through which to perpetuate its ideology and carry out its objectives. When you analyse it from a Marxist-Leninist perspective, you need to think of the form and the content. The form was the violence between Zulus and Xhosas, while the content was that the number of people who were likely to vote for the ANC needed to be reduced.

THE IFP WAS A child of the ANC when it was formed. Oliver Tambo met with Buthelezi, who had been a member of the ANC Youth League before it was banned. Their aim was to create a legal organisation inside SA. They funded the creation of the IFP to accomplish this objective. The IFP's colours, which are the ANC colours with red and white added, signalled their joint intent.

Jabulani Nxumalo, otherwise known as Mzala, was an MK member who wrote a book about Buthelezi called *Gatsha Buthelezi: Chief with a Double Agenda*. Published in the UK in 1988, many people took from the book the idea that Buthelezi was unreliable, which caused them to start withdrawing from him as a result. Buthelezi had already developed enemies among the Black Consciousness Movement and the Pan Africanist Congress (PAC), who had never regarded him as an authentic leader of black South Africans. Already in 1978, a group of some 200 youths had chased Buthelezi away from the funeral of Robert Sobukwe, the anti-apartheid revolutionary and founding member and president of the PAC.

The very same racist regime that had done everything in its power to destroy Robert Sobukwe had created the bantustan (African homeland) system. Buthelezi was made head of the bantustan of KwaZulu in 1970.

Deeply angered that youth organisations were beginning to gravitate towards the UDF in the 1980s, Buthelezi declared his opposition to sanctions. The IFP similarly came to oppose member organisations of the UDF after its founding in 1983. Buthelezi then supported the government, which wanted to destabilise the UDF.

In 1981, KwaZulu received its own police force, the KwaZulu Police (KZP). Its numbers grew rapidly, and its recruits would terrorise UDF youth who were part of a progressive force. We had a joke that KZP members were so uneducated that, if you answered in English that you were part of the 'United Democratic Front' when they stopped you to ask you about your business, they would interpret this as a sign of how educated you were and let you go. They would kill you if you said 'UDF' instead.

These initiatives geared up to destabilise the ANC should it return home to South Africa. After the ANC was unbanned, the IFP was easily able to bus people to different townships in Gauteng, including Thokoza and Soweto, as it had already put in place the required structures. They had clearly laid the groundwork well in advance of the initial attacks.

IFP members stopped me next to the Madala Hostel one day as I was walking on 3rd Avenue carrying a bag of cymbals and sticks to rehearsal. We used to see them hang out on the stoep outside Phuthuma Printers on 3rd Avenue. They would stand there and call you to them. 'Stop. Come here,' they would command.

You couldn't run away since they were carrying guns and machetes. These were young boys who were notorious killers.

A shortish guy named Sibusiso confronted me that day. I suspected that he might be planning to kill me, as he had a reputation, which many believed, for having killed a lot of people. If people responsible for war crimes were prosecuted in South Africa, he would be brought up on charges.

You checked your words carefully when you were around those people. You might say something with good intention and end up dead anyway. They used secret codes to greet and communicate with each other.

I knew what to say because I lived in the area, but still had to be very cautious.

'What language do you speak?'

'I speak isiZulu.'

'Where do you stay?'

'I stay in 4th Avenue.'

They accompanied me to my house. I was still not safe, as Sibusiso might decide to kill me at any moment.

He confirmed with one of his guys that I was from that part of the township, said 'Okay' and made a U-turn.

THINGS GOT EVEN scarier one Saturday afternoon. My wife and I were coming home after going out and were using a shortcut to go from 2nd Avenue to 3rd Avenue. A young girl who was standing in front of a house entreated us: 'Please, come into my house. I'll lock you in. They are killing people.' They would have killed us too if that girl hadn't spoken to us right then.

THE IRONY IN ALL of this was that I had come home to be a free man. Instead, I found myself in this terrifying situation. To make things more complicated, my mother had died and I needed to take care of our family. My elder sister was drinking too much, and two of my sisters had children who needed somebody as a father figure they could look up to as a model.

I was also newly married. My future wife had been with my family in Alex and decisions had been made. She had come to visit me in Zimbabwe to say that we would be settling down, and we had started planning our wedding right away.

The Inkatha upheaval had begun right after we had gone through the ceremony and celebration in Alex. We were married, but didn't know each other well. It was still a new relationship and we had not even started bonding properly. My wife and I had known each other from afar for a long time. She had been part of a group during the struggle that would come to meetings at the indigenous African church made of corrugated iron. I was one of the people heading the political discussions. That was all. It never crossed our minds that we would fall in love or come to look on each other as lifelong partners.

All of this meant that we were by no means ready for the trials that assailed us from the start.

THE KILLERS CAME UP with a campaign under which people had to pay a subscription fee and carry red pass cards in order to be protected. When they knocked on your door, you showed them the pass and they would spare you.

I was not prepared to be part of that. I wanted to fight and took out my AK. (This was before the deadline for returning them.) My sister stepped in and I listened to her. At the same time, I decided to leave Alex and find a new home. I was so determined to do this that I told certain people about my decision.

NOT LONG AFTERWARDS, however, Chris Hani sent a message asking me to come to the ANC office in Sauer Street. Naturally, I could not let anyone know I was going there: they would never have allowed it. Instead I asked the African soldiers at the razor-wire fence to let me out to go to the shop to buy bread. They stretched the fence almost flat for me.

'Sandisile, we need to know who is in charge of the killings in Alex,' Hani told me after I had arrived in his office. 'You are at the centre of the area where the killings are taking place, and in a better position than any other person in the world to work out what is going on. Don't leave Alex before you have found out for us.'

He later called me directly on the phone to say: 'Sandisile, I need to see you. We need you.' Nelson Mandela and Tokyo Sexwale were there with Hani when I returned to Sauer Street. Joe Nhlanhla, who was originally from 12th Avenue in Alex and became minister of intelligence in South Africa under Thabo Mbeki in 1999, was there, too.

I also met Chris Hani's bodyguard, Pumlani 'Ntsimbi' (Iron) Kubukeli.

Inkatha kept on denying in the local and international media that it was responsible for the atrocities it perpetrated. We had to find a way to leak accurate information to counter these declarations and justify the statements Mandela was making about the killings. This was the planning meeting intended to make this happen.

'Close the door,' Mandela began. 'Sandisile, we need you to stay in Alex right now. You must find a way to tell Inkatha that you have come to hate the ANC.'

'Why should I tell them that I hate the ANC?' I found it hard to hide my surprise.

'Because we want you to go and join the IFP.'

'No way. They will kill me, those guys.'

'You are a soldier. Without you, the ANC will never know who is in charge there. Join them. Become the secretary there. We need names. Most of the people who are warlords can't write. Go and look at the books so we can find out who the indunas are and put evidence in front of De Klerk.'

In short, he had to have the evidence needed to substantiate his statements locally and abroad.

'You are our last solution,' Chris Hani said when Mandela finished speaking. 'We have no other option.'

Nelson Mandela was commander-in-chief and Chris Hani was army commissar. I had taken MK's oath of allegiance on completing my training. In those days, you held a spear by the blade and Oliver Tambo himself pulled it out of your hand as you took the oath. Despite the danger I would surely face, I had no choice but to say yes.

THE IFP SENT TWO of their guys to me two or three days after that meeting.

'We understand you hate the ANC.'

'Yes.'

'And that you speak isiZulu.'

'Yes.'

'We know that you come from exile.'

'Yes.'

'What is your position now?'

'I hate those motherfuckers.'

'We need you at the hostel now.'

'Okay.'

I was not sure whether I would come out alive, but I went.

My older sister was angrier with me than ever before. I sometimes let her in on the bare facts of my plans when I was involved in something dangerous in case something went wrong. This time, things were so precarious I also told my wife.

'You can't go to the hostel,' my sister said.

'You can't go to the hostel,' my wife repeated.

'I have to go for certain,' I replied.

They didn't understand that my mission was for Mandela. There was no way for them to know since it was a secret.

Themba Khoza was waiting for me when I got to Madala Hostel.

Although he had a reputation as the most notorious among the Inkatha killers, I experienced him as a polite person who sat with me and listened to why I wanted to join the IFP.

'I'm told that you are a soldier,' he said.

'Yes, I was a soldier.'

'You trained in Angola?'

'Yes, I trained in Angola.'

'We're in a war here, but before we proceed, me and you, I want you to put this AK-47 back together to prove that you are a real soldier.'

He dismantled the gun quickly, and I reassembled it just as fast.

'I'm impressed,' he said, before abruptly switching the topic.

'We want to fight the Xhosas.'

'I'll do it,' I stated with conviction.

'We need you,' Themba Khoza stated.

'How do you need me?'

'These guys here can't write. They can't document their minutes. We want you to become the secretary.'

'No problem.'

He explained that I would be responsible for taking notes during the nightly meetings: 'You write the minutes. If there's anything that doesn't make sense, you tell them. You'll assist these guys in setting up the structures in terms of who comes to work when. If there's any attack against us during the meeting, you must help defend us.'

I WENT BACK HOME.

My sister asked, 'Are you okay? Are you hurt?'

'No, I'm okay,' I said.

I REPORTED TO the leaders at Sauer Street about the secret signal I had been given and on what had happened during the meeting as a whole.

'We need that book,' Mandela said. 'We need to make photocopies of the minutes, of the names in the attendance register.' We still had no proper evidence substantiating what Mandela had said about the killers. That's why he needed copies.

I got the notebook with the names in it. It showed that the indunas were responsible for the killings. I took it out, shared the information with the ANC hierarchy, and brought it back. I attended a number of IFP meetings after that as if nothing had happened. I don't know if they ever started to figure me out, but I still talk to some of those people today.

I had given Chris Hani and Nelson Mandela the information they would use to strategise.

I had done my part.

AN UNDERGROUND MK unit was put together after that to bomb the hostel and fight the IFP if necessary. There was no need for it at that moment.

I got word that the ANC leaders again needed to see me at Luthuli House. Things had become too dangerous and we needed to call an end to the pretence. I was not aware when I went to that meeting that the ANC was already busy moving my family, my furniture and my clothes out of my home without having told me about it.

They did not warn me about this – they just went ahead.

I found people busy packing when I arrived home. The members of the household were all preparing for the mandated move.

We were fortunate compared with many other people. We managed to move with our furniture and other goods, but others had had to run away with only the clothes on their backs. People who were forced to run away usually ended up taking cover in the churches and the local council offices. Our destination was a peaceful area called Buccleuch, which was near Sandton and Kelvin and not too far from Alex.

Still, the pain of saying goodbye to our home was deep and real.

Even though the ANC had organised soldiers with guns around the township, we had to be diplomatic about leaving. 'Why are you leaving, squeeza?'[5] people kept asking my wife.

'As you know, my husband is a musician,' she told them. 'He is gone for two or three weeks at a time. And when he is not around, some people take advantage. The ones who don't know him harass us.' She explained that our new home was quite close to Alex, and that she would be able to come and visit the people she knew. She told them that she would still spend some nights at home in Alex, and alternate between that and staying with her parents. When she packed, she placed stuff in boxes so no one would notice that this was a definite move.

I was furious when the ANC did not consult me before moving my family and me out of Alex. That was the last time I set foot in our home on 4th Avenue. The IFP has taken over the house even though it still is registered under our family name.

Some of their members have told me that they knew I was a king before I realised it myself, but you can't trust them.

AFTER WE MOVED OUT of Alex, Mandela started announcing that the indunas concerned were killers and provided proof based on the notebook. My training in intelligence had made it possible for me to infiltrate the IFP. Still, it had not been an easy thing to do. The information I had obtained contributed to a substantial reduction in violence. The information made it much more difficult for the government to deny that they had been supplying arms to the IFP, and to continue doing so.

The IFP ended up registering for the democratic elections, at which they were defeated. That exposé had been part of their defeat.

I soon realised that surviving this perilous incident was no permanent guarantee of safety. Despite having been officially welcomed back to

---

5   Township vernacular used to refer to a sister-in-law or a well-liked woman acquaintance.

my own country, my life could be threatened at any time.

Robben Island guys often visited me at my house on 4th Avenue in Alex. One night, I was accompanying David 'Shuffle' Jwara, an ex-political prisoner and Roots band member, to his home. He lived on 7th Avenue, not far away from me.

We were using a common shortcut via 6th Avenue. I had barely taken him halfway when security police driving a red Toyota stopped us in the street. A white guy drove while two or three black guys sat in the back. I realised that the black policemen were young askaris who belonged to the security police heart and soul, often after turning their backs on the ANC or the PAC.

It was well known that if askaris came for you, you were done for. I just kept quiet because I was still with Shuffle. I hoped he would survive while preparing myself for my own death.

Two of the askaris opened the door and trained their pistols on me before greeting me quietly in isiZulu.

'Comrade Instructor, how are you?' they asked.

I didn't recognise these guys, as I had taught a lot of people over the period during which I had been deputy head of instructors in the MK camp in Angola. I had been the oldest trainer there and had sought to assist them. I had also defended them against any person who tried to harm them.

I held my breath.

There had been one incident when an instructor abused and yelled at an elderly couple who were new trainees. They had both come to train to take the fight back to South Africa.

We later discovered that these people's children had been killed by the racist regime. I had to fight for them and approached the instructor. I was sitting at the back, but I observed what he was doing. To me, it was disrespect.

'It's wrong what you are doing. These people came voluntarily to join MK. They left South Africa to add to our numbers, so don't treat them badly. Don't do it.'

I think those askaris must have been part of the group of trainees who were there at the time.

They didn't speak to me about that incident. They just told me, 'You will survive because you had a good heart in the camp.'

'Is it him?' The white policeman behind the wheel asked about me in Afrikaans. 'It looks like him.'

'No,' answered the askaris, who'd pretended to take a good look at me. They got back into the car, closed their door and the red Toyota drove away.

Askaris were killing a lot of people in those days, but these guys remembered what had happened in Angola years before.

At that moment on 6th Avenue, their memories were why I survived.

8

BECOMING A KING

Sometime around the mid-2010s, I had a dream in which I saw three people wearing white clothing, with leopard skin over their shoulders and on their heads. These people were praying for me. The dream's content bothered me because I didn't understand it.

It kept coming back to me for a week, then a second week, and then a third. Finally, I said to my wife: 'Let me take my car and try to figure this out.' It was a Saturday afternoon and I drove to the place that seemed to be the setting for the dream – near the clinic in Alex.

I knew nothing at the time of the history of the Radebes' connection to Shembe spirituality. The Shembe have been practising their spirituality in the form of the beliefs and rituals of the Shembe Church for many years. The basis of their spirituality comes from the Radebes, a clan of the amaHlubi. More specifically, Shembe is connected to the Radebes through the area of Ntabamhlope, next to Kwasukangihlale, where my father was born.

History tells of the impregnation of a woman of the Radebe by a Shembe man, in which traditional law was not followed because she did not receive a dowry or money for damages. Because of this, the child remained hers instead of becoming the father's. My uncle, Vana Radebe, told me once that the Shembe people came to my father's home to settle this unpaid debt. In reality, the issue was never resolved.

While she was still of a tender age, this same woman had been visited by an angel who had informed her that she had been chosen to be a healer and to perform good deeds on Earth. She learned young that she had powers – and came to play an important role as a spiritual prophet, and as an angel herself, in the performance of Shembe rituals.

When I got to Alex Clinic, I saw some people and asked them: 'Excuse me. I'm looking for people wearing white clothing with leopard skin. They were praying for me somewhere near here?'

'You see these shacks?' a man answered. 'These people dress like that when they go to church.'

It was a miracle! The guy then called out to the people in the shacks to come outside. 'Hey, Msimango, come and listen to this man.'

Msimango looked at me before talking to me. Saying nothing, he shook his head.

'Why are you shaking your head?'

'What happened to your cars?'

'What do you mean, what happened to my cars?'

'Why are they crashing?'

'I don't know.'

'You'll end up poor, even more than the church mouse.'

'Why?'

'Because there's this thing you are supposed to be taking on but are not heeding.'

'What is the task?'

'You are supposed to become king.'

'Nah, don't talk nonsense to me. You are joking. I don't have time for this, man.'

'I *am* serious.'

Msimango sat down on the ground. He was talking to himself, again shaking his head and answering voices that only he seemed to be hearing. After a time, he said, 'Excuse me, Baba [Father]. Do you mind? Can we exchange numbers? All that I want from you is to avail yourself in the next two days. I don't want anything else from you. I don't want money. I will call you to say when I'm going to pick you up.

'According to the ones I'm talking to,' he explained, 'I must perform a secret ritual for you. There's a place called Msinga in KZN, where the ritual has to be carried out.'

At this point it was impossible for me to believe anything at all about being a king. 'I'm a freedom fighter,' I kept thinking to myself. 'Who the hell is this guy? This guy does not know me.' It was only later that I got to know that Msimango was a seer. At the same time, I *had* experienced the persistent dreams. It was also true that my cars kept on crashing.

I agreed to go to Msinga to undergo the ritual that changed my life.

WE TOOK OFF LATE at night and drove along the M3 highway. Including Msimango, there were three seers (sangomas) in the car.

There is a sacred mountain near Msinga called Langa Mountain, which is a place suited to the performance of sacred rites. We reached the base at about six in the morning. We tried to cover part of the ascent to the top by car. The path was too slippery, though, and we had to leave the car behind and start to climb on foot. It took us from 6 pm until close to midnight to climb to the peak.

As we were climbing, some families came out of their mountain homes and called out to us to say that there were wild animals on the mountain that would eat us. The people in those houses warned us not to go further up because of the danger. We insisted on continuing our trek.

We were climbing, resting for two to three minutes, and climbing again. Suddenly, at some point past the halfway mark, no one in the group was able to identify the path to the top anymore. My companions started to argue among themselves. One man said, 'No. We'll get there if we take *this* route.' Another said, 'If you go *this* way, it will be better.'

Although I had never been to the mountain before, I had no doubts or hesitation about how to navigate to the top. I pointed confidently and said, 'Guys, whoa. Wait. The easiest and the shortest route is *this* one.' (I later took my knowledge of where to go in a place where I had never previously been as a sign that the ancestors had shown me a shortcut.)

The other men all started to fight with me: 'We brought you here. Who are you to tell us that? You are nobody. You don't know anything. We brought you here, so just keep quiet. You are confusing us.'

They were against me because they had been to the mountain before, knew it better than me, and didn't like that I was suggesting a shorter way. Luckily, they started holding a caucus that ended with them asking me, 'Okay. You were saying. Which way do you think is the right one?'

'*This* is the shortest way,' I answered. 'Just follow me.' And indeed, the path soon became clearer and easier. It was not my doing. Clearly, the spirits of the place *were* showing me the way.

AN IMPORTANT STORY related to this mountain is that Radebe used it as an ideal place on which to breed his cattle. I've since been told that if you breed cattle in that environment, the offspring develop into the best cattle you will ever come across.

Long ago the amaBhele came to Radebe to ask for a place to stay in Msinga, and Radebe allowed them to settle next to Langa Mountain. There was another group, the tribe of the Sithole people, that came to ask for a place to stay. The Sithole started a fight with the amaBhele and in the process killed the chief of all the amaBhele clans. The amaBhele were understandably unhappy with what the Sithole had done. The Sithole wanted to resolve the matter by paying a fine in the form of cattle. 'No,' the amaBhele told them. 'If you want to be forgiven, you must raise the chief from the dead.'

That could not be done, of course. The amaBhele then issued a declaration, stating: 'Because they have killed our chief, no child of the amaBhele can have an affair with or marry anyone from the Sithole clan.' That injunction remains in force today.

The amaBhele moved from the area to a place next to Bergville in KZN. After that they migrated much further to the area that is now the Eastern Cape.

WE ARRIVED AT THE top. It was cloudy, foggy and misty on the peak. Large stones, rising upwards, were the only properly visible things there. They were similar to, but smaller than, the ones you see at Stonehenge in England. I was shortly to learn that some of them were tombs.

The three men then said they were going to the other side of the mountain and left me standing next to the stones. A second later, we lost sight of one another.

This was the first time in history that a Radebe had been sent up the mountain to perform a specific ritual in fulfilment of the journey of becoming a king. I was not yet fully aware of the impact of this trip on my future life.

A VOICE STARTED speaking to me – the voice of a divine spirit, not a demonic one. 'These men will want to take the powers you are going to be granted as King,' it told me. I only realised afterward that the sangomas might have gone so far as to kill me to obtain those powers.

The spirit appeared before me and told me what to do before the men came back. 'Take the *impepho* you have brought with you from home. Go to that hole in the rock. Repeat the things the voices tell you to say.'

Impepho is the plant you burn to invoke the spirits and invite them closer to you.[6]

I followed the spirit's instructions. 'Hide the *impepho* in the hole,' the voice said urgently, repeating the earlier warning. 'Those guys who brought you here must not see it. Do not trust them.'

I repeated the various utterances shared with me, word for word. This was an important moment for me, but I could not savour it for long.

'Take the *impepho* with you,' the voice urged. 'Hide behind the tomb that is closest to you. Burn the *impepho* there and say "One, two, three." Then nobody will touch you. Remember to take a

---

6   *Impepho* is an abundant indigenous African plant employed in various rituals and ceremonies by people throughout sub-Saharan Africa. It is used to speak with one's ancestors and is also used by traditional healers to communicate with people who have died.

photograph with your phone as you burn the *impepho*, as proof that you have performed this sacred act!'

I listened more closely than ever before. I had grown up hearing voices, but – to be honest – had ignored them. I was driven to heed the message and remain safe from the three seers' dark intent.

'It is time to speak with your ancestors,' the voice said. 'That is their instruction. You have to approach them in the same way you arrived on earth – naked. You must undress so that you can reconnect with them.'

I followed that instruction. The *impepho* burned for a while and I listened to the ancestors and engaged with them. 'It is done now,' I was told before the men came back. 'Whatever the three planned to do, it won't succeed. You are now the King because we wanted you here.'

ONCE THE THREE sangomas returned, they directed me to climb onto the shorter white stone that was at the mountain peak, telling me that this was the will of the ancestors.

I had to take into my mouth, then spit out, the African medicine they had brought with them to cleanse me; pronounce that I was the King of Kings; and state that no one was above me. I did that, after which they made cuts on my cheeks and near my eyes. I don't think they realised that my father had already made incisions on my face. They then made cuts all the way down my body. They rubbed the potion that already contained my father's blood into the cuts so that it got into my body properly and I would be a stronger king. This also ensured that if I had a child, that child would become the heir to the throne I was inheriting from my father.

'We are done now,' they declared.

THIS FIRST OF THREE rituals led to my becoming initiated as King. The second group of rituals was carried out at our homestead. And the third ritual came in 2015, when I was presented to the people.

The three men had a directive to speak to the four corners of the world, to say that I was to be the King above all Kings in Africa.

It would be my responsibility to notify the ancestors who control our kingship if a potential successor were born. I would give my recommendation concerning my successor, after which they would reach their decision. Luckily, they came back to me to say that my son must be the one to follow me on the throne.

I performed the ritual for my son Khosi when he passed through puberty. The ancestors told me to give him an impala skin rug. This was to symbolise that he was the crown prince and the heir to the throne. They also told me that he will be ready to take over on the day I go to join the ancestors. I have three sons, and Khosi is the youngest.

Ultimately, he's been chosen by God. We don't choose.

I CAME DOWN THE mountain with the others. You came across houses in various spots as you descended the lower slopes. Women came out from their homes and started ululating, 'Lilililililili', in praise of what had happened. They were overjoyed we had made it back.

I didn't know why this celebration was happening, as no one besides the men who had accompanied me up the mountain had known that I was going to undergo the ritual. According to local tradition, whoever goes up there does not return.

Residents of that area told me, again and again: 'No man can reach that summit and come back alive.'

But I had.

I WAS SUFFERING FROM a degree of shock despite my safe return. Msimango, the seer from Alex, sought to calm me and convince me that all was as it should be. 'If, in the next two months, you are not called to take over the kingship, if your family from Natal, from Msinga and Estcourt, does not convene a meeting, you can come and choose anything in my shack and keep it,' he promised.

We returned to Alex immediately after those events. That same week, there was an ANC Subcommittee of International Relations meeting at Luthuli House near the centre of Johannesburg. Baleka

Mbete-Kgositsile, former secretary general of the ANC Women's League, was co-chair of the meeting.

'You resemble two people I know, but let's talk about it after this meeting,' she said to me when I entered the venue. She had never said anything of the sort to me during the months she had known me.

'Can we continue with this at my home?' she asked me after the meeting ended. She didn't have a meeting agenda for me, and I was uncomfortable enough with the situation to decide that I wanted my wife and my sister to accompany me. My wife did not want to go. She said, 'If you die, it'll be much better if you die alone so that I am able to pursue your case without you.'

As for my sister, she was ducking and diving.

'What is this thing, man?' I asked. 'Now that I'm a king, you don't want to talk?'

I went there without them. When I arrived, I found a lot of people. And cars. And the police. They had brought their own seer, too. They were all there for me.

'Hey man, you've got the wrong guy,' I said.

The meeting room had a big table with different people seated around it who started to ask me questions. It was like an interrogation. Baleka locked the door, put the key in her pocket, and declared: 'Let's sit down and talk. We're not going to leave here until everything is resolved. There is food here. There's a toilet. You're not going anywhere until we're satisfied that all our questions have been answered.'

'Where were you born? How were you born? Who is your father?'

'I don't remember all that, but you know what? The best person to answer these questions is my sister,' I told them. 'Ask if you can speak to her and put her on speaker phone. She's older than me. She knows better.' They called her and she obliged with all the facts at her disposal. A more serious trial awaited me after the group indicated its satisfaction with her answers and I was finally allowed to go home.

I was told one final thing would confirm whether or not I was a proper king: the traditional medicine that only a king can drink without harming himself. This was a family medicine, and I needed to go back to KwaZulu-Natal to drink it there. If I truly were a king, I wouldn't die on the spot. If not, I would die instantly.

I wasn't sure about this at all. 'Eh, should I go there or not?' I asked my uncle Vana. The elders had no hesitation: 'You want to show that you are your father's rightful son.' My father had never had any boys besides me. Only four daughters. In their minds, I had to defend the position that I was his genuine son. They were even asking me funny questions, such as: 'How sure are you that you're your father's son?'

Although I knew that I had been carried by my mother, I didn't know how to answer those other questions. It was a difficult experience to face because human beings are driven by cultural ethics. If you were told as the only son to acknowledge your father as your sire, you had no option but to do so.

At the same time, I had not fully accepted the kingship scenario so unexpectedly thrust on me. I was still uncomfortable with the whole story. As a Marxist, I was totally opposed to the institution of royalty. An understanding that 'This is who you are' still needed to be imprinted on me.

This was why I was having conversations with God, the main gist of which was: 'You are far removed from things that you are supposed to do here on earth. You have disappointed me.'

God's words moved me towards that missing understanding. Also, at a certain level – and as was fairly typical with me – I simply didn't care. 'Let them go to hell, I'm going to drink this potion,' I decided.

WE DROVE TO NATAL around Christmas. It was the first time I was going to my father's home. He had fled Natal because his enemies wanted to kill him. I was a grown man who was coming home. Vilakazi, the chair of the house of Bhungane on my father's side, accompanied me.

I remember that I had forgotten my jacket. I had a chill because it was extremely cold outside in the middle of the mountains. After we'd reached our destination and alighted from the car, we stood outside the houses we were visiting as people sang the traditional praises for a king. This took up to a couple of hours. 'Hey, I think I must look for a stone to sit on,' I said at some point. I did this just to get the people to say, 'Better let them in. This guy's been freezing for a long time.' Having finally noted my discomfort, they invited us into one of the homes.

Some old ladies were sitting on the ground as we walked in. 'No, this one is ours,' they declared when they saw me. 'We recognise him from when he was young. We watch our children here. We know them very well. He is ours.'

'That's not enough,' the men said. 'He must drink.'

At around seven that evening, they told me that they were going to say a prayer. 'Do you see this medicine?' they asked me. 'If you are not our child, it will not produce any foam. But if you are from this house, the foam will appear.'

'That's proof number one,' they told me. 'Number two is when you drink.'

Nobody stayed in the house after that. They just put the medicine down and left it there until the early hours of the morning. At about 4 am, they opened the door to see if the foam had risen and left a lit candle next to it. In the morning they woke us all up before again opening the door of the house.

Foam was clearly visible above the liquid, but the elders were unconvinced. 'It's not enough foam,' they declared before coming to a decision. 'Let's go and drink it,' they said.

They gave me my half.

I started drinking the potion slowly.

They began to put heavy pressure on me. 'Drink! Drink! Drink!' they yelled.

It tasted just like ordinary medicine. They told me to keep sitting and observed me. Nobody spoke to me, they were just talking quietly among themselves. I sat there and they sat. Finally, my uncle Vana spoke as the leader of the group: 'You know what? Let's go and vomit this medicine. You *are* one of us.'

They gave me a fighting stick because I had not died. The stick looked like a knobkerrie with the round top that men have traditionally used to protect themselves against animals and enemies. They put that stick in my hand. A ritual was carried out at about six in the morning. They went and fetched a goat to slaughter and started singing praise songs. Everybody from different corners of the area was there, coming from near and far to greet their new king.

WHEN I GOT BACK to Alex, my sisters failed to display the surprise and relief I'd expected. That's when I found out that they had known all along that I had a certain destiny. 'Hey, we didn't want to tell you that you were a king because we were protecting you against getting killed,' they told me.

They started putting everything in context for me: 'As king, you have to be aware of your blood. When you were small, your father put some medicine in your blood before taking some of it away from the kingdom. This was to preserve the bloodline. If a contender for kingship tolerates the medicine, like the one they gave you at your father's home in Natal, their kingship will be one of unity. If they don't, they cannot rule.'

That was what had happened to Langalibalele, my father's would-be rival. He had been unable to withstand the potion's power. He swallowed it and started vomiting right away. It did not kill him, but it did paralyse his mouth. Even though that man wanted to be king, he was not a king.

My sisters had known since I was born that I was a king and had never told me. They had kept it a secret for fifty years to protect me. I fully began to adopt my new leadership role the day they spoke to me and confirmed the truth.

I OPENED THE SPEECH at my coronation in 2015 by saying that I was just a normal human being. I also told everyone present that I was there to do the job I had promised myself and others I would do, and that I wanted to make a start on it before it was too late. That job was to make sure that unity prevailed in Africa. That was the goal I had decided I must dedicate myself to for the rest of my life.

There is now no other path for me. I trust what my father asked me to do. I also know that I'll be lost if I don't execute what my father asked for. I don't want to become known as a lost angel because the doors won't open for me when I need to go to the ancestors. I'll be one of those angels that roam around in the sky without a mission. I don't want to be like Lucifer, the fallen angel who was unable to go back home.

The good news is that God gave me a child to be heir to the throne, and that he chose him to continue with the legacy I am trying to build. My son Khosi knows about his intended role. I told him that he would accede to the throne before he turned fifty years old, the age I was when I learned about my destiny. I am King Bhungane III of the amaHlubi, and he will be King Bhungane IV.

Khosi already has special knowledge. He has a power I don't have: the power to stop the rain. I've seen him do it on various occasions and in different locations. When people came to clean our house from top to bottom last time, the guys could not do a proper job because it was raining. Khosi went outside to stand in the rain and I heard him uttering words that I could not understand.

'What are you saying?' I asked.

'No, Dad, it's my secret,' he replied. 'I'm sorry. This is between me and God.'

'I can't tell you,' he repeated, as he continued to stand in the rain with his back to me.

Hardly two or three minutes later, the rain made a *woosh* sound and stopped altogether.

That's power.

MY JOURNEY AS A comrade taught me how people who don't have a connection with God behave. It taught me enough about human beings to conclude that you cannot trust them. You can only trust God. What happened with the ANC and the land in South Africa is a case in point.

I also learned that there is a difference between indigenous kings and those who are indigenous and spiritually driven at the same time. (There are also those Western-style kings like Misuzulu, who are not indigenous seers with the power to communicate with the ancestors.)

This hard-won knowledge has served me well on my new journey. Before I was born, my mother was told, 'Your son will be a son of the world. He will go to jail and into exile. But this will all be part of a learning curve for him, as he needs to understand how cruel, dishonest and selfish people can be. He'll go through all of this suffering so that he can become a king – a king who knows the difference between right and wrong.'

That is what has happened to me.

Bayete.[7]

---

[7] Zulu royal greeting, more recently used as a compliment to any favoured persons.

INDEX

A
Alexandra Action Committee (AAC) 92
Alexandra Civic Association (ACA) 92, **93**
Alexandra Property Owners' Association 11
Alexandra Student League (ASL) 94
Alexandra Youth Congress 92
Amandla Cultural Ensemble 16, 23, 109, 116, 131, 141, 149, 150, 152, 156–157, 160, 162, 164–167, 171, 174
ANC Subcommittee of International Relations 193
Ayob, Ismail 98
Azanian People's Organisation (AZAPO) 105
authorities
    Adjudant (senior guard on Robben Island; sellout; spoke Xhosa) 65, 71
    Afrikaner policeman (Special Branch, seen with Swazi's partner) 88
    Afrikaner warders (armed guards transporting prisoners from Leeuwkop to Robben Island; peed on the prisoners) 45–46
    established instructors (abused some of the recruits at ANC camp in Angola) 129
    Francistown police (suggested Khulu find Ntate Nthithe) 114
    Hunter (Robben Island guard) 63–64
    head of prisons in South Africa (interviewed Khulu when he first arrived on Robben Island) 47–49
    head of Robben Island prison (bully; antagonised Khulu) 67–69, 76
    Jefferson (platoon commander in Botswana) 122, 123, 125
    judge (presided over Khulu's trial before he was sent to Robben Island) 40
    Kleynhans brothers (agreed to take Khulu off Robben Island without chaining his legs) 69, 70
    Lebogang (head of MP police; said Khulu couldn't be guilty of rape) 132
    local commissioner of police, Botswana (requested written biographies from Khulu and comrades) 113
    Mathumbu (Robben Island guard, announced Khulu was being released) 79
    Nxumalo, General (South Africa; explained legitimacy of UNITA) 118–120, 137
    police (at Khulu's trial; told him to say 'hi' to Mandela) 42
    professor of political science (at

Khulu's trial before being sent to Robben Island; talked about bombings) 41
prosecutor (at Khulu's trial before being sent to Robben Island; recommends a 20-year sentence) 41
Security Branch 82, 86, 88
Security Police 36, 87, 184
Sibeko (Alexandra policeman; pulled out of his vehicle and stabbed on 18 June 1976) 7, 34
Sishi (got the woman Khulu was accused of raping to speak at the trial; possibly murdered for his actions) 133, 134
Special Branch 169
two policemen (toKhulu to court every morning for his trial) 40
two white policemen (June 1976; ignored the crowd of students) 34
warders (Robben Island; hours-long strip searches) 58
white Afrikaner (followed Khulu in Lusaka) 146
white policeman (drove two askaris who stopped Khulu in Alexandra, but didn't know who he was) 184, 185
white prison warder at Leeuwkop (helped Khulu dress neatly) 44

B

Baard, Frances 92
Baloyi, Principal 36
Bands and singers
African Jazz Pioneers 171
Anchors 7, 19,
Bayete 172
Big Hennie's Band 25
Dark City Sisters 171
Flaming Souls 7, 19, 20
Ibrahim, Abdullah 165
Jennifer 159, 162
King Sunny Adé 172
Mango Groove 25
Movers 7, 19, 20, 24
Osibisa 172
Rita Marley and the Wailers 172
Roots 170–172, 184
Sakhile 172
Santana and Mbongeni 159
Sis Esther 159
Third World 172
Bapela, Connie 102
Bapela, Obed 11, 30, 37, 38, 92, 93, 94, 97, 99, 102, 103, 105
Biko, Steve 31
Black Consciousness Movement (BCM) 31, 176
Black People's Convention (BPC) 31
Bob, Dr (kidnapped in Angola) 142
Buthelezi, Mangosuthu Gatsha 176–177
Buti, Rev. Sam 36

C

Communist Party 45
comrades and acquaintances
Boogie Man (betrayed by traitors in the ANC in exile) 88–89
Charlie (drunk at the airport in Addis) 163–164
Deddy (went into exile with Khulu) 113
Elce (Chinese store owner) 17
Faku (wanted Welcome Msomi's room for his informant) 131
Fort (worked in the kitchen with Khulu; co-accused of rape) 132–134
Gumi (Ngomso) (personal tutor on Robben Island) 11
Keiko (from Japan, staying with Khulu when the violence started in Alexandra; 1991) 173
Lungi (Lebogang's wife; had a child with Sithole) 131
Mangosuthu (felt that guard duty was beneath him) 144–145
Michael (medical student at Groote Schuur and old friend of Khulu's) 72, 81
Mike (gave Khulu and Naude a lift to Harare) 116

INDEX

Mokgalabi (prisoner on Robben Island who allowed the guards to take him off the island in chains) 70-71

Moss 37 (protested with Khulu in Alexandra in 1977)

Msimango and two other seers (seer who prophesies that Khulu will be king) 188, 189, 193

Naude (comrade and friend) 91, 92, 94, 101, 102, 104-109

Nhlanhla (chose to stay at Protea Police Station rather than risk being called a traitor) 89

Norman (Elce's son; skilled in martial arts) 17

Ntwaza (lost the Alexandra secondary school bell running away from the police on 18 June 1976) 35

Papa (lost his passport at the airport in China) 161-163

Pesco (veterinarian who acted as a doctor for Robben Island inmates) 62

Pro (commander of Angola's security cluster) 131

Sarah (doctor at Groote Schuur and old friend of Khulu's) 72, 81

Sensei from Soweto (Khulu's childhood karate instructor) 15

Sibusiso (IFP member with a reputation for murder) 177–178

Simon (Khulu's childhood karate instructor) 15

Sithole (camp commissar, Angola) 131, 132

Stalin (prisoner on Robben Island) 78

Swazi (member of MK) 88

Taylor (member of Amandla Cultural Ensemble) 161-163

Tekere (member of the ANC Youth Congress) 108

Thabo (MK officer in Angola) 144-145

Tso Tso (member of Khulu's youth group) 30

Vilakazi (chair of house of Bhungane on Khulu's father's side) 195

Vladimir (Khulu's instructor in the Soviet Union) 128

Congress of South African Students (COSAS) 33, 92

Cultural Resistance Movement 165

D

Dean, Izzy 123–125
Dimitrov, Georgi 54
Diradingwe, Michael 95
Dolores, Anne 104

F

Fazzie, Henry 53
Funde, Eddie 164

G

Gangs
   Dirty Heroes 6, 7
   Msomis 6,
   Panga Men 7
   Spoilers 6
   Ten Slaughters 6, 7
   Young Ones 6
Gwangwa, Jonas 23, 150-151, 157, 162, 171

H

Hagar, Dr (Angola) 142
Hani, Chris 108, 125-127, 146, 149-153, 179, 180, 182
Hlatshwayo, Albert Linda 'UmKhulu' 8
Hlatshwayo, Sophie 8, 12, 13

I

Imbokodo 115, 116
Inkatha Freedom Party (IFP) 105, 173, 175, 178–181, 183
International Red Cross 64, 66

J

Jomo, Cyril Pitso 113
Joseph, Helen 83
Jwara, David 'Shuffle' 171, 184

K

Kathrada, Ahmed 99, 158
Kgasoane, Banza 25
Khawuleza Cultural Ensemble (KCE) 30, 32, 105

Khoza, Gerald 20
Khoza, Themba 181
Kiki, Joseph 8
Kotane, Moses 99
Kubheka, Muzi 18, 103
Kubukeli, Pumlani 'Ntsimbi' (Iron) 179
Kwela, Allen 24

L

Langalibalele (not the rightful heir to the throne) 4, 197
Lebese, Sandy 53
Lewis, George 25
Lifakane family 10

M

Mabena, Ronnie 171
Mahlangu, Solomon 94, 119, 173
Makgale family 10
Makgothi, Jingles 30, 81, 91, 92, 105, 106, 110, 111
Makhene, Blondie 19
Mamasela, Joe 87
Manana, Joe 169
Mancheck (former criminal planted by the racist regime in Quatro prison camp) 87
Mandela, Nelson 6, 11, 38, 42, 53, 59, 60, 63, 71, 74, 87, 114, 126, 147, 158, 159, 167, 179, 180-183
Mandela, Winnie 83, 97–99, 167
Mangope, Lucas 91
Manzini, Mrs (head of Minerva High School) 90–91
Manzini, Phumuza 91
Marks, JB 99
Martins, Dikobe Ben (Dikobe wa Mogale) 30
Masekela, Barbara 170
Masekela, Hugh 166, 170, 172
Mashego, Collins 20, 24
Mashinini, Tsietsi 32
Mashoba, Delisa 83
Masondo, David 18
Mass Democratic Movement (MDM) 87, 88, 165
Matanzima, Kaiser 51
Mayekiso, Moses 93, 96, 97

Mbatha, Baba 95
Mbeki, Govan 53–54, 60, 126
Mbete-Kgositile, Baleka 194
Mchazo, Dr (Alexandra) 13
Mehlomakulu, Themba (Welcome Msomi) 130
Mgwenya, Violet (nee Hlatshwayo) 8, 12
Mhlanga, Curtis 171
Mike, Bra (Reverend Mike) 93
Mlambo, Johnson 69
Mlangeni, Andrew 173
Moeketsi, Kippie 24, 171
Moerane family 10
Mogale, Lebogang 131, 164
Moisi, David 46
Mokoena, Aubrey 83, 98
Moleketi, Jabu 116
Molokoane, Barney 119, 122, 130
Morgan family 10
Mphahlele, Es'kia 30
Mseleku, Bheki 171, 172

N

National Union for the Total Independence of Angola (UNITA) 111, 135–140, 142–144, 152
National Union of Metalworkers (NUMSA) 93
National Union of South African Students (NUSAS) 31
Ndaba, Queeneth 171
Ndaba, Sam 102
Ndlovu, Curnick (Tata Nyanga Umthakathi) 73–75
Ndlovu, Hastings 33
Ndlovu, Vusi 15, 16
Ngcobo, Sipho 52
Ngidi, Justice Hlomuka 89, 169
Ngwenya, Jabu 83
Nhlanhla, Joe 179
Nhlapo, Meshack 113
Nhlapo, Welile 169
Nkadimeng, John 83
Nkobi, Thomas 167
Nkosi, Zakes 25
Nthithe, Ntate 114
Ntuli, Ncane 'MaBIDa' 94

INDEX

Nxumalo, Jabulani, aka Mzala 176

O
Ogen family 10
Omar, Dullah 70

P
Pan Africanist Congress (PAC) 16, 30, 51, 52, 67, 69, 75, 77, 176, 184,
People's Armed Forces for Liberation of Angola (FAPLA) 120, 134, 139, 140, 143, 144
People's Movement for the Liberation of Angola (MPLA) 120, 137, 139, 140
Phahle, George 29
Phahle, Levi 24, 29
Phahle, Principal 28
Piliso, Mzwai 125

Q
Qumbela, Mountain 78

R
Radebe, Gaur 11
Radebe, Khosi 193, 198
Radebe, Mabel 3, 82, 197
Radebe, Margaret(wife) 6, 95, 173-175, 178, 181, 183, 187, 194
Radebe, Mariam (Khulu's mother) epigraph, 1, 5, 7-10, 20, 21, 35, 38, 40-42, 64-65, 80, 82, 84, 85, 98, 178, 195, 198
Radebe, Ntombi 8, 20, 171
Radebe, Samuel 8, 9
Radebe, Vana 187, 195, 196
Ramogkadi, Martin 83, 84, 90, 94, 103
Ry, Short 7

S
Seathlole, Kerry 84
Selepe, Dumi 22–23
Selepe, Fana 21-23
Serote, Wally 169
Sexwale, Tokyo 179
Shabalala, Vincent 103, 122
Shabangu, Johannes 45, 46
Sibeko, Sipho 'UmCaravan' 45
Sibisi, Thami 30
Sis Tlaletsi 133
Sisulu, Lindiwe 169
Sisulu, Walter 38, 39, 74, 158
Sithole, Thembinkosi 57–58, 61–62
Sizani, Zweli 107
Skhosana, Toto 34
Smith, Solly 153, 154
South African Communist Party (SACP) 53, 54, 128
South African Council of Churches 66, 83
South African Students' Movement 31
South African Students' Organisation (SASO) 31, 33
South West Africa People's Organisation (SWAPO) 114

T
Tambo, OR 5, 42, 61, 99, 157, 166, 176, 180
Thabane, Frank 'Machini' 171
Thabo, Sam 7, 19, 20, 24
Transvaal High Command 83, 84, 113, 127, 131
Tshabalala, Ma 12
Tshwete, Steve 119, 120
Tutu, Bishop Desmond 37

U
Umkhonto we Sizwe (MK) 73, 86–90, 92, 103, 105, 108–111, 117–119, 121, 122, 125, 133–138, 144, 146, 149, 158, 170, 176, 180, 182, 184
United Democratic Front (UDF) 83, 88, 92, 106, 108, 160, 165, 176, 177
United Nations (UN) 73, 78, 90, 114
United Nations Refugee Commission 114
University of Makana (Robben Island) 56, 72, 78
unnamed family members
    aunt's husband John (manager for The Movers) 7
    father 3–5, 7, 187, 192, 195, 197
    maternal grandmother 5
    sisters (Khulu had one older sister, Mabel, and three younger sisters) 8, 10, 19, 178, 197
    sons (Khulu has 3 sons) 193

unnamed strangers
   askaris (don't betray Khulu because he had a good heart) 184–185
   beautiful coloured woman (nurse at Groote Schuur who fetched Michael) 71
   Cuban doctor in Malanje 130
   Guinean woman (daughter of the president of Guinea) 154–156
   guy arrested for sleeping with a white woman 133
   guy from KZN (died after a bullet was inserted into his weapon) 130
   guy from Stinkwater (Khulu and Naude stayed in his shack) 91
   hostel dwellers (murdered mostly Xhosa people in Alexandra) 173, 174
   informant and his family (working with Faku in Bostwana) 131
   Katangese guy (shot in the genitals and begged to be killed) 135
   man approaching the house (killed during the violence in Alexandra in 1991) 174
   man at hospital (asks Khulu at Groote Schuur why he was arrested) 71
   man in Alexandra (helped Khulu find Msimango) 188
   man at hotel (tried his luck with the daughter of the president of Guinea) 159
   manager at Farm Fare (gave Khulu's mother free chicken to help her feed her children) 9
   MK recruit (lasted just three days at Viana transit camp) 121
   old ladies (at Khulu's father's house; recognise him as a member of the family) 196
   two people wearing balaclavas (waiting in Bramley to kill Khulu) 110
   person who backed Khulu's father (supported his right to be king) 4
   prisoner (on Robben Island, told an insulting joke) 51–52
   questioners (told Khulu he had to drink the potion to prove he is king) 196
   Russian instructors in Malanje (advised Khulu to get treatment in Eastern Europe for his injured hand) 130
   second prisoner (got offended by first prisoner's joke) 51–52
   son of Hashe (shot by firing squad after being found guilty of rape) 132
   Swazi's partner (betrayed Swazi) 88
   taxi driver (Alexandra, 1991; killed people, even children) 174
   truck driver (refused to give Khulu a lift from Francistown police station) 115
   two Afrikaner youths (casually shot a child; Alexandra 1991) 112
   two elderly women (asked Khulu why he was dressed in prison clothes at Groote Schuur) 71
   two white guys (Bramley 1991, rescue Khulu from an assassin) 110, 111
   white woman (shines her brights for a moment, allowing Khulu to see his assailants) 110
   woman radiographer (gentle touch when examining prisoners) 66
   woman who saves Khulu (before his arrest, evading the police) 36–37
   woman who testifies (confirms that Khulu is not guilty of rape) 134
   woman with a baby on her back (Alexandra 1991, shot and killed) 174
   Xhosa prisoners (circumcise other Xhosa prisoners as per custom) 46
   Young people on their way to Israel 174

V
Van der Merwe, John 94 **N**

W
Wadikapetso, Tshepo 126
Walter, Commissar 135
Weinberg, Sheila 83